MW00510743

A WINNING LEGACY

A WINNING LEGACY

RON BISHOP

AN AUTOBIOGRAPHY

ISBN 13: 978-0-9788748-3-4
ISBN 10: 0-9788748-3-8

Published in the United States by
Synergistics Inc.
Roanoke, VA
First Edition: October 2006

Library of Congress Cataloging-in-Publication Data

Bishop, Ron, 1945-
  A winning legacy : an autobiography / Ron Bishop. -- 1st ed.
     p. cm.
  ISBN-13: 978-0-9788748-3-4 (hardcover)
  ISBN-10: 0-9788748-3-8 (hardcover)
  1. Bishop, Ron, 1945- 2. Basketball coaches--United States--Biography. 3. Clergy--Biography. I. Title.

GV884.B575A3 2006
796.323092--dc22
[B]

2006033691

Printed in the United States of America
10 09 08 07 06   1 2 3 4 5

DEDICATION

To Ashley, Lex, Allyson, and Chloe
I hope you will always be winners in life.
To my incredible daughters, Robyn and Rhonda
I am grateful you have enriched my life
with your love and dedication.
To my two sons-in-law
I am grateful for your love and leadership.
To my faithful wife, Pat
Thank you for your love and devotion. Without you,
I would have no legacy worthy to be read.

CONTENTS

Contents

Reflections on Winning | 151

Reflections on Ministry | 171

A Faithful Finish | 205

PREFACE

John Shulman is an energetic young coach who became head basketball coach at UT-Chattanooga in his early thirties. I spent time mentoring John in spiritual matters. Both his parents died before John was 26 years old. John and his beautiful wife have three sons. What this means is simple: John's wife and his three sons never knew John's parents.

I can relate with those young boys. My father's parents both died before I was born. I NEVER KNEW THEM. Many years have passed, and I still know absolutely nothing about my father's parents. He and his siblings have passed. I will never know a lot about the Bishops, and that still bothers me.

When I had open heart surgery in 2005, I thought a lot about that. As a Christian, I was prepared and ready to die; however, I had a fighting will to live because of my family. They were my main reason to live.

Paul said, "For me...to die is gain!" Wow, I know that I have a whole lot to gain by dying; yet, God was not finished with me. Paul also stated, "To live is Christ." I want to live to impact others for Christ. I feel needful, but to be with my family drives me to live.

As I lay in Memorial Hospital, I had a strange compulsion to write my story in order to leave my legacy for my grandchildren. I did not want to die and have my young babies know nothing of their grandfather Ron.

That night, I planned to write the story of my life for my grandchildren. The more I wrote, the more I began to enjoy the project. Thus, I decided to expand it and write a book.

The world isn't looking for another book to read. The Bible is "the greatest Book ever written" and people ignore it. Why should I write a book? I am just an old preacher who happened to coach.

My vision for this project centered on my grandchildren. I want them to know Christ, to live for Him, and make Him known. I want them to know me, feel my heart, and be challenged by my values, commitment, and love for God and His Word.

My legacy will soon be forgotten by the masses of people. Sixty years after I am dead, no one will remember me! My desire is that my daughters, their children, and their children will be aware of their heritage. That's why I knew I had to write my story.

As a coach, I enjoyed fame in the southeast. My picture was in newspapers, my face on television. People recognized me. I was elected to four halls-of-fame. I was named national coach of the year twice. This fed my ego.

Five years after I retired from coaching, I went to a game at the university where I led four teams to national championships. Normally, I got free admission to games. However, one particular night, a freshman girl at the gate told me the price of admission was five dollars.

I asked her to check and see if my name was on the pass list.

"What is your name?" she asked.

I knew at that moment that fame is fleeting. People forget—and most do not care any more.

I paid to watch the game that night. I was no longer obsessed with my significance. I could never do anything to impress the girl at the gate. My legacy means nothing to her and that is o.k. with me.

What is important to me now is to leave a legacy with the people I love. I want my bloodline to know me and follow me as I have followed the Lord. I want to make an impact upon several generations of my family.

This is the reason I began this project. It has been expanded to challenge coaches, athletes, and leaders. I hope you enjoy the stories. As you read, keep in mind, you have a legacy. Make a mark on your family. Let them know who you are and what your life is all about.

It is sad that John's sons will never know their grandfather. I never knew my grandfather Bishop. By God's grace, I will leave my legacy with my grandchildren as a challenge to "acknowledge Him in all their ways and He will direct their paths."

• • • •

I am still coaching! My family is so special to me. I enjoy coaching my grandchildren. No, I do not push them to play sports. I never pushed Robyn or Rhonda. If Ashley, Lex, Allyson, or Chloe want to know how to shoot a basketball, I will teach them. I went to their soccer and baseball games before they began school. To be honest, I really enjoy just hanging out with them.

Ashley is the oldest. She is very studious and asks a lot of questions. She is a lot like her dad. She is very conservative and has good business sense. Ashley is creative and loves to write. She would make a good lawyer. She loves to argue and is analytical.

Lex is a real man. From birth, he always had broad shoulders and a barrel chest. He will always carry weight, but looks like a linebacker or lineman. Lex is tender and intelligent. He is a step slow and is flatfooted. He may never be a great athlete, but he loves the Lord, and I believe he will serve Christ.

Allyson is very athletic. She was born premature and will always be slightly built. She is a good runner and is our fastest grandchild. Allyson seeks to please and has a wonderful heart. She will be popular, but I believe she will choose the right values in life.

Chloe is the baby, and she is a doll. She loves to entertain and doesn't mind being the center of attention. She is very pretty—and she knows it. She is the little prissy one in our family.

In June 2006, we took a family vacation to the Dominican Republic. It was the first time Robyn, Greg, and Allyson had been overseas. Robyn never went on a mission trip with me. Rhonda went many, many times, beginning when she was eight years old. It just wasn't Robyn's thing to do, and I never pushed her.

I think the vacation in the DR was the greatest trip I ever made overseas. It was special because we were all together on a family mission trip. I was so happy that we could be together on mission for God as a family in a foreign country. That was so neat! My family got to go to the spot on the planet where God called me into ministry. They saw our mission training center, orphanage, and dental/medical clinic. They also attended a worship service where I preached. I took them to a sugarcane village where we do a lot of humanitarian work. I hope they caught a small glimpse of my heart for the world.

My family means more to me than any team I ever coached. Coaching championship teams brought a lot of satisfaction to my life. Mentoring my grandchildren to be champions for Christ is the ultimate ministry for me. Now you see what I mean when I say, "I am still coaching!"

A WINNING LEGACY

INTRODUCTION

"Winning isn't everything!"

"It doesn't matter whether you win or lose, it's how you play the game."

I've heard these statements for years. I understand the context in which they are stated. Sometimes athletes seek advantages that are unfair and unlawful in order to win. Society puts such an emphasis on winning. However, winning is OK. While winning may not be everything, "wanting" to win is everything. And yes, it is how you play the game, but winning also matters.

I love to be around winners! When I fly in a plane, I don't want a loser as pilot. When I needed heart surgery, I investigated to find a surgeon who had a winning record. When I need legal counsel, I look for lawyers who win.

I grew up in the era of Vietnam. Sadly, our country allowed that war to become a political war; therefore, we pulled out before victory. For the first time, our military was not allowed to win. As a result, we lost fifty-thousand American soldiers and we lost the war. In a new millennium, a war is raging in Iraq. People again want to pull out, walk away, and allow the terrorists to win. I believe our objective in war ought to be to WIN!

Jesus Christ was a winner! When tempted by Satan, Jesus used the Word of God to gain a major victory in the wilderness. Again, Satan sought to keep Jesus from going to the cross. He lost! Yet, it was on the cross that Jesus appeared to be a real loser who ultimately lost His life. But remember, Jesus said that no one could take His life, but He could lay it down and He could pick it up again. Even when He died and was buried for 3 days, He appeared as an ordinary person who lost a huge battle. However, on that Sunday morning, Jesus Christ walked out of that grave as a victor over death and Hell. Wow, what a winner!

Sometime later, the Apostle Paul would declare that thanks be to God we have "victory" through our Lord Jesus Christ. In the book of Romans, Paul declared that Christians are "more than conquerors" through Christ. And when one reads the last chapter of the Bible, we know that we are "on the winning side." No wonder Jack Wyrtzen, an internationally known evangelist, signed his letters, "On the Victory Side".

Winning matters!

As a young athlete, I cared about winning. I trained hard, and I played on high school teams that won. Late in college, my college basketball team lost a lot of games; it was horrible. However, my teammates and I made a commitment to work, practice hard, and spend extra time in individual workouts. Three years later, we turned a 3–20 losing program into a 22–8 winning record. We learned that the American dream is about sweat, work, commitment, and other old fashion values, which translate into success.

Winning matters! And winning is OK!

Now as I look back over my life, I see how easily I could have been a loser in the real world. I could easily have chosen to be an alcoholic. You could say that I had a predisposition to alcohol since I was raised in a home of alcoholics. But God had a plan for me! Early in my life, I understood that there are a lot of winners and losers. I had a deep passion to succeed, to contribute, and to be a true winner. I made a conscious choice to become a Christian, to give my life to Christ, to follow His Word, and to commit my plans, goals, gifts, dreams, and aspirations to Him.

Once I made my decision to dedicate myself totally to God, He began to favor me in ways I never dreamed. The Bible says if we honor Him, He will honor us. It states that the steps of a man who follows Him are "ordered of the Lord." When one acknowledges Christ, He directs his steps.

When I say that I had no advantages, it is an honest fact. I never achieved status with God. I never inherited opportunities to advance. I never pulled myself up by my bootstraps. I am what I am by the grace of God. It is the Sovereign God who made me a winner. I never deserved it, but I do appreciate what God has done. I can declare that I am a winner! That is not a statement of boasting or pride but a declaration that I am the recipient of God's grace.

Sometimes people ask me how I would succinctly describe myself. If I could write my own epitaph on a headstone in the graveyard, it would read:

"RON BISHOP, A WINNER IN LIFE WITH A PASSION FOR THE SOULS OF MEN AND LEGACY TO IMPACT OTHERS."

Winning in life is the only thing that counts! I have told teenagers for many years that decisions determine one's destiny—not dreams but solid decisions. Because of my early home life, I decided that I would seek to excel. I had a passion to become successful. I wanted to be a true winner.

For me, winning began in the classroom. When I was in the fourth grade, I was a below average student. After a long talk with my aunt Sadie, I decided to strive for better grades. From the fifth grade until high school graduation, I was an honor student.

My quest for success was most evident in sports. Sports gave me the confidence, security, and recognition that was needed in those turbulent teenage years when I could have easily chosen a different path in life. However, I had been around so many losers. Because I saw so much failure in the lives of people, I was driven with the urgency to become a good citizen, a productive person, and a winner in the big game of life.

I believe winning is a choice. A true winner is one who seeks to excel and at the end of the game knows that he gave his best. In an athletic contest and life, things are not always equal. However, when a person maximizes his potential, he wins in spite of the scoreboard. Many years ago, I made a choice to pursue a path of success. With all the intensity of my heart and by the grace and sovereignty of God, I decided to push myself and avoid mediocrity in order to become a winner in life.

I am glad that I made that choice!

From this book, I want you to know me personally, understand my purpose in life, feel my passion, and glorify our Lord. His plans are greater than all of ours, and He delights in making us WINNERS!

BORN LOSER

CHAPTER 1

WINNING IN SPITE...

I was listening to Founder's week from the historic Moody church in Chicago. The speaker was giving a great expositional sermon from Judges. He was speaking concerning the call of Gideon to ministry. In chapter 6 and verse 15, Gideon said, *"...behold, my family is poor in Manasseh, and I am the least in my father's house."*

Now that is getting close to the bottom! But God had a plan to deliver His people from the Midianites. The plan called for using Gideon, whose family was heavily influenced by worshippers of Baal, a false god.

God told Gideon to destroy the altar to Baal, which his father had built, and to build an altar to Jehovah God. In Judges 6:27, we are told that Gideon did as he was commanded. He was obedient, but he did the work AT NIGHT, because he was so afraid of everyone in his father's house.

Because of His promises, God was going to save Gideon's neck anyway. Nevertheless, Gideon wavered in his faith, and he asked God to demonstrate by a sign—the sign was to be the use of a fleece. So in verses 36–40, we read the rest of the story!

It was an interesting sermon. The three principles gleaned from Gideon's experience caused me to reflect on my own call to ministry.

The three principles are as follows:

1) God calls inadequate people to incredible ministries. (Judges 6:15)

2) God calls fearful people to fruitful ministries. (Judges 6:27)

3) God calls doubting people to daring ministries. (Judges 6:37)

Looking back over my 40 years of ministry, I can identify with Gideon: inadequate, fearful, and full of doubts. Why would God ever call me? What could I possibly do? How can it be done?

"Ronnie Bishop is gonna do what?"

"You gotta be kiddin', right?"

"A preacher? Boy, God must be getting desperate! But Ronnie?"

Yeah, I remember those responses during my senior year at Blacksburg High School in northern South Carolina. Truthfully, it really wasn't what I had planned for my life. However, I did have a plan! You have to plan for your life when your parents are alcoholics. I knew that if I wanted to go to college, enter a successful career, and "turn out right," I had to have a plan.

I guess most people figured I would become a drunk like my parents, following in my dad's footsteps. Like father, like son!

But not me. I really loved my dad. He had a great career in electrical distribution. He was a supervisor for an electrical contractor in Charlotte, North Carolina, which was forty-five miles north of Blacksburg, a town of two-thousand people just inside the South

Carolina line. He was a great dad, but he had this bad alcohol problem. So I learned to hate alcohol.

I have <u>never</u> tasted alcohol. Now that is a powerful statement, but for me it was never a temptation. Neither was it a God-thing! I just knew how it ruined my parents' health, hurt our family, and caused us to be surrounded by a lot of <u>losers</u>.

Nevertheless, the older people in my town figured I may go off to college and come back a drunk. After all, I did have a predisposition to alcohol dependency, since it was in my genes. Psychologists would have never given me much of a chance to get out of Blacksburg sober.

I grew up in Blacksburg fearful, embarrassed, insecure, and envious of all my friends. I grew up hating bootleggers, home brew, "white lightning," and everyone who drank alcohol. Dysfunctional, confused, and wild marked my boyhood. Weekends were never normal. Holidays were never normal either, especially Christmas, the Fourth of July, New Year's, Labor Day, or any holiday that called for celebration.

My maternal grandparents were extraordinary people. E.J. and Luna Mae Hardin had eleven children, six boys and five girls. Marvin was the oldest boy and my mother was the oldest girl. They lived on a 150 acre farm in Blacksburg South Carolina. The farm was primarily used to raise livestock and cotton. All the children were hardworking people.

My grandfather Hardin was a quiet man. He became a deacon in the First Baptist Church and a school trustee. In addition to raising cotton, grandfather Hardin worked a third-shift job at a textile mill. Later in life, he opened a gas station and sold groceries on his property.

Grandmother Hardin was a great Christian lady. She was the spiritual backbone of the family. She also worked hard on the farm.

Grandmother Hardin was a beautiful lady with Southern charm. She had strong convictions and set high spiritual standards for her children and grandchildren to follow.

However, the family was far from perfect. Marvin, the eldest son, answered the call to preach. After beginning to study for the ministry, he became an alcoholic. He gave up the ministry and died an alcoholic. Yates was also a son who struggled with an alcohol problem. As a young soldier, Ansel had a drinking problem, but became a model citizen in the city of Blacksburg, serving as a town councilman. Darvin owned a building construction company. He and E.J., Jr. were solid Christians and were deacons in their church. E.J., Jr. was elected several times to the county school board. Ralph was the youngest son. He lived in a sanatorium for two years after having tuberculosis. He never married and became the youngest magistrate ever elected in the state of South Carolina.

All the boys, except Marvin, settled in Blacksburg and raised their families there. None of the boys ever divorced their wives. They had thirteen children.

Mom was the eldest daughter, the fourth child born in the family. Mary and Kacky were born next. Mary had only one child, Frankie. She owned a beauty parlor in Blacksburg. Kacky was the wild one. She divorced her husband after years of physical abuse. They were alcoholics and later she became addicted to drugs. She abandoned her children and disappeared after a second marriage. A lot of mystery surrounded her eventual death.

Flora Ann was the fourth daughter. She eloped while in nursing school in Shelby, North Carolina. Flora Ann was a little headstrong. Her husband Frank was an alcoholic, and they were farmers in Florida. In spite of a tough marriage, they struggled through tough times. Frank and Flora Ann lost four children. Two were born dead. While one lived a few months, their son, Jamie, died on his sixteenth birthday. She was a very resilient, tough woman. Frank later died of cancer after they lost their farm. Flora Ann purchased a motel, which she later lost. Most of her life was filled with suffering, financial difficulties, and sorrow.

Sadie was the youngest daughter. She was a lot like grandmother. Sadie was strong in spiritual commitment and a true Southern lady. Her husband, Vernon Sanders, was a politician. He became the mayor of Gaffney, South Carolina. (If you have ever traveled I-85 and seen the peach shaped water tower, Vernon Sanders built that while serving as mayor of Gaffney! It is ugly and topic of a lot of conversation.) When Vernon died of a heart attack, many attempted to get Sadie to assume his office. She could have done it. Sadie was a popular person with a lot of wisdom, charm, leadership, and people skills. However, her son, Vernon, Jr., became the mayor while in his early twenties.

Sadie had a lot of influence on me! She gave me a lot of advice and guided me during critical decisions of my life.

The girls had eleven children. Mom, Mary, and Sadie stayed in the Blacksburg area. Of the twenty-four grandchildren, seventeen of us lived close together in Cherokee County. We got together a lot for picnics and cookouts. Many of us gathered every Sunday after church for Sunday dinner at Grandmother's house.

The cousins who were closest to me were Son, Ernie, and Frankie. Son was Marvin, Jr. I was the oldest grandson and only a few months older than Son. Ernie was one year younger. We played on the high school football team together. Frankie was the son of Mary, and an only child. To be honest, Son, Ernie, and I picked on Frankie a lot.

Our Sunday afternoon football games were brutal. We played tackle football, without pads. Usually, someone walked away in blood. We loved to make one of the younger ones cry.

I will always treasure the memories of life on the farm and those Sunday afternoons. We had a close family. I never remember a Thanksgiving, Christmas, or Easter when we failed to gather at Grandmother Hardin's house. During those days, we almost always had thirty-seven people on the farm.

True, we had our family problems. Grandmother reminded all of us how important our family name was in the community. My grandmother and grandfather had a name that was respected. She wanted to protect that name. I will always appreciate the legacy of my grandparents. They raised eleven children, mentored twenty-four children, and later took four of those grandchildren into their home to raise. I was one of those grandchildren. Those 3 years in their home helped mold my life, shape my values, and cement my resolve to live for Christ.

• • • •

I did have a plan, a goal, and a passion. I wanted to be an engineer, make money, and have a nice house and a good family. I wanted to become a good citizen, contribute to the community, and go to church. I just wanted to be normal and live the American dream.

But how? How could I do it? I knew I would get little help from home. My dad made good money, but how could I go to college, when they could barely make ends meet? Dependency on alcohol strains a family budget.

Suddenly, a light came on in my young brain. Get a scholarship! Yeah, that's it. But how? I knew my grades were only average. To this moment in my life, I didn't have much motivation; therefore, I had little hope.

But you know what? I could run fast. I could throw a football, and I really loved basketball. Soon sports became the passion of my life. I began to play in the backyard, the neighborhood, and the school. I tried out for every sport in its season. Sports would become the savior of my life. Through sports, I could realize my dreams, reach my goals, and work the plan for my life.

I soon learned every social need I had could be met through sports. I had learned that everyone has four basic social needs:

1. To be loved
2. To gain recognition
3. To feel secure
4. To belong

I knew that none of these needs were being met at home. I felt alone, insecure, abandoned, and worthless. Because I could run faster than my friends, shoot a basketball, and throw a football, I was suddenly THE man in the seventh grade. Girls liked me, guys envied me, and I was beginning to love myself.

I even began to love school, teachers, and even the principal. I started studying more and became a member of the school Beta Club (National Honor Society).

Then it happened! My dad came home to tell us he was being transferred. I just made the team and now we were going to move. It didn't happen just once, but over the next two years, I attended three different schools in three different states.

There was no stability. By the time I got adjusted to another school and their teams, we moved. To make things worse, the alcohol problem of my parents was at a peak.

I hated my life. I hated my parents. I hated school. When I began to hate myself, I knew I was at the breaking point of my life.

Was I going to abandon the plan? Was I going to give up, quit? What about college? What about a career? What was I going to do with my life?

Summer came and that meant a week on the farm with my grandparents. Every summer, I spent a week living with my grandparents. They lived on a 150 acre farm. They had chickens, cows, pigs, mules, five barns, hayfields, and cotton—lots and lots of cotton!

The farm was a retreat, a place to get away. You see, my grandparents were very religious people (Godly is a better word!). My grandparents drove into town three times a week to attend the First Baptist Church. They prayed before every meal and read the Bible every night together. They tolerated no cussing, fussing, or drinking—if you wanted to go to Heaven. And if you wanted to be a good church member, going to movies, dancing, and playing cards were out also.

Even though they raised eleven children of their own on the farm, they still loved to have most of the twenty-four grandchildren come and visit during the summer. Being with my grandparents for one summer week prior to going into the ninth grade was about to change my life, forever.

I had a great time gathering eggs, plowing with the mules, chasing the cows, and being with the best Christian people on earth. This home was a piece of Heaven. At the end of the week, I DIDN'T WANT TO LEAVE!

I began to scheme. But how? What would be the reaction of my parents? Grandma and Grandpaw were old. Why would they want to take in a 14-year-old after raising their limit? I knew I didn't want to move anymore. I knew I wanted stability in school. I knew I wanted to play ball so I could go to college on a scholarship. And I dead sure knew I still hated the smell of alcohol.

16

Really, it was dramatic. One night after prayer, I just asked my grandparents if they would consider letting me live with them. I told them that moving so much hurt me in school. I reasoned that a sports scholarship would help me get to college, but I couldn't continue in sports if my parents kept pulling me out of school. I can't really say they lovingly embraced the notion, but at least they didn't fall out of their chairs. They didn't have a stroke, so I knew there was a chance.

I never mentioned alcohol. You see, my grandparents never knew their daughter and son-in-law were drunks. They never saw it. Maybe they suspected it because of whom my parents called their friends, but they never saw it. Since my parents deeply respected them, they would never go to the farm with alcohol on their breath.

Selling the whole idea to my parents was easy. They were already feeling guilty about dragging me out of schools so much. They knew my grades were suffering. They knew I loved to play ball, to be on the team.

So in August everyone came together and a decision was made. I was leaving Mom and Dad, my sister, and two brothers. I was going to the farm. Even the smell of pigs on a hot August day was better than the stench of a "cool one." My aunts and uncles may not have favored the idea, but the oldest grandson was HEADED TO THE FARM.

CHAPTER 2

LIFE ON THE FARM

Life on the farm was great. Even greater was the fact that I loved school. Blacksburg High School was vital to reaching my goals. I had great friends such as Myra Harris, Agnes Martin, Jane Wilkins, Nancy Wilson, LaRue Cobb, Rusty Cabiness, and Johnny Harper. Jerry Moss was crazy, but I loved being with him. Some people thought Marvin Bishop was my brother. Wayne Brown didn't play ball but he was my idol. Wayne was the kind of person whose personality was contagious. He was "Mr. Perfect" and the standard by which all of our parents judged us. Wayne and I went to church together at the First Baptist Church. We both trusted Christ at an early age and were baptized by Rev. James Stokes on the same day. Diane Patrick was beautiful and Myra Harris was the Wayne Brown among the women.

I just loved being at BHS. I made the football team, the basketball team, and the track team. As a ninth grader, I won the mile run at the Piedmont Conference meet held at Wofford College.

By the time I reached my junior year, I was a huge success in sports. I was a starter on the football team, which was very successful. Oddly, I struggled in basketball because it wasn't as important as football at BHS. In track, I never lost in the mile run!

I was right on schedule to get that scholarship. I was working my plan! My grades were good enough to put me into the Beta Club, our school honor society. I loved everybody and they loved me.

However, I really struggled as a Christian. No, I don't mean I was bad. Grandma made sure I didn't go to movies and dances. Church going was never an option. She made me read the Bible and pray.

I could date girls on Friday and Saturday nights; most of the time it was double dating with Rusty Cabiness. Although I didn't have a car, Grandma did have eleven children so my aunts and uncles got regular calls for borrowing the weekend ride.

Oh, one other thing! I had to be home by 11 p.m. Wow!! After the game, there wasn't much time to be romantic, when I had to take a date home and make it to the farm before 11 p.m.

I was saved at the age of nine, after hearing a man preach about hell. I knew I didn't want to go there! My pastor explained John 3:16 to me, and I gave my life to Jesus Christ.

Nevertheless, I grew very little spiritually in high school. Outwardly, I conformed to all the rules of the farm. I never drank, nor was I ever rebellious. I was good but not godly.

I had a game plan! I wanted a scholarship to college so I could be a success in life. Sports were my ticket to success. My life revolved around a piece of leather filled with air and my ability to run. I filled a trophy case full of medals, ribbons, and trophies.

Life in Blacksburg was special. I enjoyed living in a small town between Charlotte and Spartanburg. Knowing everyone in town had its drawbacks, but being like a close-knit family outweighed all the negatives. The people of Gaffney looked down on us, but we were proud of who we were. We could go to Shelby as well as Gaffney for shopping and weekend entertainment.

Special times of the year brought a lot of fun. I will always remember Halloween. It was the time when all of us who lived in the county would descend upon our small community and join our friends in the annual trick or treat madness. In essence, it was more about "tricking." We ran all over town in little bands, turning garbage pails upside down, tearing down stop signs, and lobbing cherry bombs at the police station with a slingshot. There weren't enough policemen to spoil our fun. I remember one year someone took our city limits sign to Union, about twenty-five miles away. After retrieving the Union sign, they swapped them and posted them in the ground.

Through a lot of harmless fun, we made a mess in our little town but created a lot of memories.

The county fair in Shelby was another annual event we cherished. Someone would always get a big flatbed truck, fill it with hay, and we would hayride all the way to the fair and back. Highway 18 had a lot of hay on it, and we had a lot of fun.

Shelby seemed to be the place for Blacksburg teens to go on the weekend. It was only 15 miles away, and we went there to play putt-putt, ride go-carts, go bowling, or eat at Bridges' Bar-B-Q. It was a place to take a date or just hang out with the guys.

I remember one bowling trip we took to Shelby. There were six of us: Rusty, Jerry, Kenneth Putnam, Tommy Cooper (my cousin), Ernie, and I. We had bought some cherry bombs, and Jerry Moss was determined to show his mischievous nature. As we drove up Highway 18, Jerry spotted some black guys swinging in a tire swing. As we approached the house, Jerry lit a cherry bomb and threw it at the boys in the swinging tire. As we looked back, we saw the cherry bomb explode and boys scatter. It was not a racist "hate crime." These boys just happened to be black. Jerry would have done it if they had all been white or brown. We almost wrecked the car in laughter.

After bowling that night, we started back home. When we were halfway to Blacksburg, Tommy shouted and said that we had to go back.

"Go back, where?" I asked.

"We've got to turn around and go back to the bowling alley," Tommy said, as he lifted his size twelve foot up onto the front seat, showing us his bowling shoes that belonged to the bowling alley.

Living in Blacksburg was close to our two state universities, the University of South Carolina and Clemson University. Occasionally, a group of my buddies would go to a big ACC football game.

I remember one occasion when we traveled to Clemson to see the Tigers play. There were five of us, and Jerry Moss was driving. That alone was cause for concern. Just before we got to Clemson, we stopped to get some gasoline. Jerry went to the restroom while we pumped the gasoline. Since the restroom was occupied, Jerry frantically looked for an alternative.

"Look! I can't believe that boy is going to the restroom right next to the building!" a stranger exclaimed.

After paying the bill, we quickly got in the car to drive off. Jerry noticed a cat crossing in front of us. I knew Jerry would hit the cat, but he mashed the pedal to the metal and spun out right over the cat.

It is truly a wonder that we grew up in the little town of Blacksburg without police records. There was never a dull moment.

By the end of my junior year in high school, I was so popular that I was elected president of the student body at BHS. I even had a prominent role in our junior class play.

No, I am NOT full of myself! I am just telling my story. It is the story of an inadequate boy who was fearful and doubting just like Gideon in the Old Testament. It is the story of a boy who had every excuse to be a loser but decided to be a winner. It is the story of a boy who planned his life but was soon to have a powerful encounter with God. This encounter with a sovereign God made me realize a spiritual truth. You see, I found out it really wasn't about MY plan for my life. God revealed that He had His plan for my life. It wasn't about success; rather, it was about surrender. If I was willing to follow Him, I would soon learn the real joy of victory. I was on my way to becoming a real winner.

Life in the 1960s was pretty cool! We had Be-Bop music, Bass Weejuns, glass pack mufflers in '56 Chevy's, madras shirts, carefree days at school, and Civics class. Mrs. Biggers taught civics, and she was intimidating. She looked mean and commanded complete compliance. I mean this lady was TOUGH!

Going into my junior year, there was a small setback for the family. One of Grandma's daughters was divorced and having a battle with alcohol and drugs. She had three children: Tommy, Yvonne, and Susan. All were younger than me. Grandmother decided that those grandchildren needed to come and live with her. Her other children were not excited, because Grandmother had raised eleven children of her own, and now she was taking four grandchildren, including me, into her home.

To be quite honest, I wasn't happy about it either. I mean, my grandparents had only three bedrooms in the farmhouse and a total of four beds. Because of their age, my grandparents slept in separate beds. You figure it out, and you'll know why I wasn't a happy camper. However, I knew it was the right thing to do.

Our football team had won ten games the year before. We were good and we knew it. Coach Bill Fisher, assisted by James Moseley, built a dynasty in the upstate. I was to be the captain and quarterback.

However, prior to our season opener in September 1962, something happened that completely and drastically changed the direction of my life.

The Blacksburg Ministerial Association planned a citywide crusade to be held in our football stadium the week before our season opener. Now, I was very religious but a weak Christian; I really didn't know how this would fit into my schedule. We had just come off two-a-days in that hot, humid weather. To be honest, I was tired.

I knew I had no choice about going to the first service of the crusade. The opening service was Sunday night. After all, my grandparents always took me to church on Sunday night. However, I got into a "mild" argument with my grandmother about going EVERY night. She knew absolutely nothing about two-a-days. Why, she didn't even know if the football was pumped or stuffed, and I was dead sure that she didn't care.

Actually, that first night was going to be awesome. Arriving at the stadium, I saw some of my friends and teammates who attended other area churches. So we climbed the steps to the top of the stands, where we thought we could check out the crowd and be far away from the preacher.

The evangelist was Dr. Jimmie Johnson from Fuqua Springs, North Carolina. He was well-known throughout the South and a personal friend of Dr. Billy Graham.

As the service began, I was impressed with the size of the crusade choir, composed of singers from area churches. I mean, this wasn't going to be bad after all.

Then it happened!

My mom and dad walked into the stadium and took a seat in the stands! Seeing them was a punch in the heart of my belly. I thought they were likely drunk. After all, it was still the weekend, and they got stoned every weekend. Knowing they were intimidated me.

I did not hear a word that Dr. Johnson spoke. My eyes stayed fixed on my parents. I just hoped they would not do anything that would embarrass me. I had worked so hard to build my reputation. I had a plan for my life, and it was going quite well. One bad move in that crusade could be devastating to me.

Dr. Johnson concluded his sermon and made an appeal for sinners to come and receive Jesus as Savior. The choir began to sing "Just As I Am." My parents moved from their seats and walked to the front.

I just knew they were drunk! You see, I saw them try so many times to break the grip alcohol had on their lives. I bolted from where I was standing with my friends on the last row and swiftly moved toward my parents. I felt I needed to be there and stabilize them, so they wouldn't fall in front of all my friends.

As I approached my mom and dad, I saw them weeping. They cried a lot when they were drunk; but to my amazement, they were sober. The

Holy Spirit opened their eyes to see their lost condition. They embraced Jesus as their personal Savior. Now they were forgiven, free, and forever new creatures in Christ.

I was crying with them. I was hugging them. Now I didn't care about my friends or what they thought of me or my selfish plans. I asked God to forgive me for being so proud, so self-centered, so focused on Ronnie Bishop.

It was so shocking and unbelievable. In my wildest dreams, I never saw this coming. As a 17-year-old athlete, I saw the power of God and knew that God was more than a nebulous spirit floating in the air! He was real and could do the impossible.

Wow, what a scene down front at the crusade. People came to us. We were all crying. The town drunks just got saved.

The principal of Blacksburg High School came to embrace me. Robert Clary was also a deacon at the First Baptist Church, where I was a member. Mr. Clary felt I should meet the evangelist. Proudly, he introduced me to Dr. Johnson and told him that I was captain of our high school football team and president of the student body.

I thanked Dr. Johnson for coming to Blacksburg to preach (even though I didn't hear a word he said that night). I told him how happy I was that my parents were saved.

Dr. Johnson looked at me and asked a very unusual favor. He asked me if I would come forward every night of the crusade when he gave the invitation. Why, I hadn't even planned to come every night! Now everything was different. I said yes. I would have cut cartwheels down the aisle for this man.

He explained to me that many times God speaks to people about their spiritual needs, but they hesitate to go forward because of the intimidation of the crowds. He was right! I would have never gone forward that night if I had not seen my parents move.

So each night during the invitation, I left my place and went forward. My friends were watching me and wondering. I am sure that they thought I was losing it! They knew I was bad, but not THIS bad! Some were concerned that I just wasn't getting it. Nevertheless, when the choir began to sing "Just As I Am," that was my cue to get down to the front.

For the first time in my life, spiritual things made sense. I was totally committed to Christ. As a matter of fact, playing football on Friday night made little sense to me.

The season opener was to be in Pacolet, South Carolina, on the Friday night during the crusade. Even though I was team captain and quarterback, I just felt I shouldn't walk away from what God was doing. So I went to Dr. Johnson.

"I just feel I should be here at the crusade on Friday night," I said to the evangelist. I felt he would understand and know that I really meant business for God.

"Oh, no! You can't do that," Dr. Johnson exclaimed without hesitation. "That would be a terrible testimony to your team. Go to the game, but get up on the bus and testify to the team and invite them to the crusade on Saturday."

Wow! That was wise counsel. Dr. Johnson knew how crazy our little town was about football.

What Dr. Johnson didn't know was that I had never testified before. I didn't know what a testimony was. Suddenly, I felt a cold sweat run through my body.

I can't! I won't! He will never know. I tried to reason to myself. What will my friends think of me? Satan really played games with my mind. I couldn't give a testimony on the public school bus headed for a public school game to people who knew me. Why, I was sure they would laugh and call me a preacher.

What was wrong with me? Why did I feel so intimidated? I was never a follower, but I was the leader. My friends did not dictate their lifestyle on me. Was I going to wimp out on God? Was I going to be weak just because this was about spiritual things?

Sitting on the bus as we headed to the game, I had a war going on in my heart. I can't and I won't. I should and I will. Finally, I stood up, looked around, and began to give the first testimony of my life.

"I guess you guys have been hearing about the crusade in the stadium," I began. Actually they had been hearing about me going forward every night.

"Mom and Dad got saved and I have surrendered my life to Christ. Tomorrow night I want all of us to go together to the crusade!" I finished the testimony and sat down. I didn't care what they thought of me. I refused to allow myself to be so weak that my peers would control my life.

We won the game that night. As a matter of fact, we won seven games that season, losing only two. We lost to Jonesville 7–6 and Woodruff 14–6. In the Woodruff game, I sustained a broken bone in my throwing hand.

On Saturday, I headed back to the crusade at the stadium. Twenty players joined me.

Dr. Johnson preached and gave the gospel. The choir began singing "Just As I Am." Yep, I went forward again! However on this night, twenty teammates followed me. It was incredible.

Boy, I am glad that God gave me the confidence to not put God in a box. Suddenly, the spiritual things in my life became my first priority. I was the president of the student body. I was the captain of the football team. God gave me a sphere of influence, and I was determined to stand up for the Lord. Rather than be intimated, I decided to be the intimidator. My friends were going to hear about Christ. They had to deal with that, because I wasn't turning back.

After the crusade in August, I made a big decision. I decided to move back with my newly converted parents. They were renting a house across the street from the First Baptist Church on Main Street in Blacksburg. After all, getting away from booze, bootleggers, and homebrew was the main reason I left home in the first place. Now that Mom and Dad were changed by the gospel, I desired to be with them, my sister Paula, and my two brothers, Eddie and Johnny. I was excited to be HOME!

After a few months, we moved to the country. We rented a two-story house across the road from Jane Bridges, my classmate.

Meanwhile, back at school, I was having a blast. Grades were good and football was great. We went 7–2 for the season, and I was the MVP as a quarterback. I took a role in our senior class play. Even though I was determined to live for Christ, it never caused my popularity and leadership in school to diminish.

Conflicts always arose, however. For instance, as a student leader, I was supposed to attend the "sock hops," which were dances after football games. I knew my grandmother had strong convictions that dancing was taboo for a Christian. However, I went anyway. I never learned to fast dance, but I loved slow dancing, for obvious reasons. I never stayed long at a dance, however. I always felt uncomfortable and thought I was staining the Hardin family name.

God was working His plan in my life. I struggled spiritually. I still did things that were wrong. I was weak. However, I was growing. I made progress, and I knew it would all come together soon. I wanted to live for God, but I was weak in the area of peer pressure. I was struggling to reach that point of total surrender.

CHAPTER 3

GETTING IN THE GAME

I hated sitting on the bench. When an athlete gets a taste of "being in the game," he never wants to be sidelined. Oh, I was always a team player. Every athlete has to spend some time on the bench. Bench players are certainly part of the team. They ride the same bus, wear the same uniform, and follow the leadership of the same coach.

But when you get in the game, something explodes inside. You feel the adrenaline of the moment. You feed off the emotion of the crowd. You are in a position to earn the affirmation of your coach.

However, for years I sat on the bench for God. I refused to pay the price, to push toward excellence, and pursue spiritual things with a passion.

Then it happened!

"Ronnie, God has laid on my heart to take you on a trip to the Caribbean," Dr. Johnson stated. "Think you can go?"

I was stunned. First of all, I didn't know what "laid on my heart" meant. Secondly, if God told him that, it was obvious I could go.

"Sure, when?" I replied.

"Well, it will be in January, and I will send a couple of friends to pick you up in Blacksburg. They will drive you to Miami to join our group."

Boy, was I excited. God had saved my parents, used me to go forward every night of the crusade, given me a testimony, and saved some of my teammates. Now I was going to the Caribbean.

Where is the Caribbean anyway? How do you properly pronounce it? How is it spelled?

You see, living in Blacksburg, we didn't have much to do. We could go to Shelby to bowl, play putt-putt, or skate. We usually drove nine miles to Gaffney to meet girls. A real splurge was a trip to Charlotte, North Carolina, which was 40 miles to the north. But now, I'm going to the Caribbean islands.

I was amazed how excited my little town got when they heard about my trip. The local Rotary Club had me come to speak. Churches invited me. People were giving me money. Ronnie was going with a famous evangelist on a trip overseas.

I was not prepared for what was about to take place in my life!

Early in January, two men came to pick me up, just as Dr. Johnson had explained. Tommy Steel and Gerald Schelling were in their late thirties. I was shocked to learn that one was a radio evangelist and the other was a pastor. I knew that I had to be on my best behavior.

Before boarding a British West Indian Airways DC-3 in Miami, I met the rest of the group. There were FORTY preachers. They all wore suits. My idea of "having a good time" when I was a teenager was not going anywhere with forty preachers. Besides, I didn't even own a suit!

Some of the preachers were famous, but I had never heard of any of them, including Dr. Jerry Falwell. I felt so intimidated by this clergical crowd.

Our first stop was Montego Bay, Jamaica. From there, we bused across beautiful mountains to Kingston. Along the way, we visited missionaries. We stopped in Mandeville and had a preaching service in the courthouse, which was packed with people. Dr. Johnson asked me to share a word of testimony.

I just couldn't believe this was happening. Here I was in Jamaica with forty preachers, visiting with missionaries, and sharing my faith in a courthouse. How could I ever explain this trip to my friends when I got home?

The next country we visited was Haiti. On the western side of the island of Hispanola, Haiti sits as the most impoverished country in the Western Hemisphere. With 97 percent illiteracy and an average income of $200 per year, the Haitian people live in despair, destitution, and darkness.

One visit to Port-au-Prince, the capital, was like stepping back in time a century. The streets were filled with potholes. The people were dirty and starving. Scores of little children followed our American delegation through the streets, begging for money. Giving one person a dime could spark a riot.

I saw people living in houses made of sticks, tin cans, and cardboard boxes. The smell in the air was a stifling stench.

I discovered that these African emigrates, brought here originally as slaves, were very religious people. However, their religion was voodoo. Sheltered as a teen back in the Carolinas, I never had any idea that there were people living in countries where the state religion was devil-worship.

The next day, Dr. Johnson announced to our group that we were going to the mountains to visit a national church. This little excursion was going to shatter all my dreams, goals, and plans that I had made for my life. I was about to step into two different spiritual worlds.

Our first stop was at a voodoo village. The houses were made of mud with thatched roofs. Children were naked and oblivious to thoughts of shame. Men gathered chickens, killed them, and drained the blood into a vat over an open fire. Later, a witch doctor gathered the people for a ceremony. The adults drank the blood, supposing that it would draw them closer to demonic spirits. Several were drunk, and all began to dance.

Never in my wildest dreams could I ever have imagined that such things were happening in the world. I was overwhelmed by the hunger, the ignorance, the poverty, and the spirit of darkness. And to think, all of this was happening just two hours by plane from our American shores.

I cannot begin to tell you how God was stirring in my heart. I was just a teenager (and not very spiritual), but I knew that God was working on me. I knew I would never be the same.

Later, we drove to the mountains to conduct a church service. Wow, was this a contrast to the voodoo village! There was still poverty and illiteracy, but it was strikingly and distinctively different.
The building was small but packed with people. They sat for hours waiting for the American preachers. Through open windows (sorry, no air-conditioners), I saw people stretching their necks to catch a glimpse. People sat on limbs in trees to get a good vantage sight for the service.

The service began with a bang. The singing was beyond imagination. At the top of their voices, the people began to exalt God by praising the name of Jesus. I cried and I laughed. I saw worship from the heart. I knew I was in the presence of people whose love for Christ was preeminent.

Sitting there, I also learned another great truth. Remember, these people had absolutely nothing: no cars, no bathrooms in their homes, no running water, no money, and very little food. Yet, they were HAPPY! How could people with nothing be happier than my American friends who had everything? How could that be possible? The answer is simple: For the first time in my life, I saw Christians who found Christ to be sufficient for every need.

I knew in that service that I must help people. I could not educate them, or feed them, or bring enough possessions to spoil them, but I sensed that I could do something.

God was calling! He was calling me, but I had a plan for my life. My goal was to Go to Furman, play ball on scholarship, get a quality education, and make money. After all, this was the American dream. Now all of that seemed so selfish. God was calling me to take the Bread of Life to a hungry world. He was calling me to bring the light of the Word to penetrate the darkness of sin.

Would I continue to sit on the bench or get IN THE GAME? Would I make my plan work or work out the sovereign plan of God for my life? Was this just a coincidence that Dr. Johnson asked me, the only teenager, to come on a trip with forty preachers? You've got to remember that my idea of having a good time wasn't going anywhere with forty preachers!

Suddenly, I came to the front, knelt, and died to all my dreams, goals, and ambitions. I gave Him my <u>soul</u> to take to Heaven when I was nine. That night, I gave Him my <u>life</u>. It was not easy because I wanted to hang onto my life. That night caused me to understand that Jesus also died for my life.

From that day, I never wanted to sit on the bench. I got a little taste of the excitement of being in the game for God. Being on the team, wearing the uniform of Christianity, and sitting on the sidelines was no longer an option. Now I was in the game!

From Haiti, we traveled to the Dominican Republic. Never in my wildest dreams did I foresee that someday the Dominican Republic would be a focal point in my ministry. We landed in Santo Domingo and stayed at a Holiday Inn.

When I was a young boy, I loved the New York Yankees. Mickey Mantle, Whitey Ford, and Bobby Richardson were the dominant team in major league baseball. In the 1960s, Bobby was the most outspoken Christian in professional sports. In fact, He was the first pro athlete I remember who took a stand for Christ. At every opportunity, Bobby used his platform as an athlete to share the message of Christ. That really impressed me.

I found out that Bobby had shared the gospel with the Alou brothers. Felipe, Manny, and Jesús are Dominicans. Our host missionary shared with us that Felipe lived near the Holiday Inn. I asked the missionary to show me exactly where Felipe lived. Since this was January, I knew he may be home.

During a free day, I determined to go to Felipe's house. I had three semesters of Spanish, so I felt this would be a good time to use it. Chance Melton was a good teacher, but I was not ready for this. You see, our Spanish class was not really an option. It was the only foreign language taught, and I needed the credit to go to college. Spanish was like an event. It was fun! We had parties at Mr. Melton's house. Rusty, Jane, Nancy, Wayne, and all my "cool" friends were in that class. I wished I had taken Spanish more seriously. I never envisioned that someday 30 percent of our population would be Spanish-speaking. Likewise, I never foresaw traveling to Hispanic countries each month.

Armed with my head full of Spanish, I left the Holiday Inn in search of the house where Felipe lived. Mr. Melton never told us how fast the Hispanics spoke the language. To a southern boy with a slow drawl, I had difficulty understanding what I was hearing. I did catch enough words to know it was Spanish.

I found his house and knocked on the door. Suddenly, he appeared.

"Mr. Alou?" I queried.

"Yes," he replied in English, with a heavy Hispanic accent.

"I'm Ronnie Bishop, and I just wanted to meet you."

"Sure, come on in the house," Felipe said, as he humbly opened his home to this wide-eyed Carolina teen.

What a day! We talked about his career with the Giants, but I really wanted to hear about his testimony with Christ.

"Yes, I accepted Jesus as my personal Savior in my hotel room on opening day," he stated without hesitation. "Someone gave me a tract explaining God's offer to me of eternal life. Here, this is my personal testimony on a tract. Take it with you and pray for me."

As I looked at that tract with his picture in a Giants uniform, I knew God was doing something special. I thought how awesome it is for Christian athletes to stand up and speak out. Coaches and athletes could have an incredible impact on young people and a culture that is crazy about athletes and sports.

I left Felipe's house that day with a new role model. I was not a pro; but as an athlete, I needed to stand up and reveal that Christ was my personal Savior.

In the hotel that night, I was reading in the book of Romans. In chapter 1 and verse 16, Paul wrote these words:

"For I am not ashamed of the gospel of Christ...."

That day, I adopted that verse for my life. I was determined to take a bold stand for Christ. I was willing to pay a price for being committed to His cause, but I would no longer be ashamed to proclaim my relationship with Him.

I have never regretted that decision. I know that I have not always been a model Christian. I know that I have failed. After all, I am a sinner like everyone else. But Jesus became the priority of my life at the age of 18. I determined to know Him and make Him known to others. One thing was for sure: Now that I was in THE GAME, I would never be ashamed.

A FORMULA FOR WINNING

CHAPTER 4

DECISIONS
DETERMINE
DESTINY

Decisions determine the destiny of your life, not your dreams. January 1963 was critical for me. I had a plan, but now it was shattered by my decision to follow Christ. This was a personal decision of obedience. I knew it would affect my friendship with some people. I knew it would ultimately affect who I dated.

As an athlete, I knew the value of decision making. As quarterback in football, I had to make decisions. Even running track demanded decisions. Later, when I became a head basketball coach in college, I always built my team around a point guard who made good decisions. Being tall is a great asset, but no team ever won championships without a heady point guard whose decision making controlled the outcome of a game.

I knew when my trip to the Caribbean was over, I had to go back to Blacksburg High School and face all my friends. I knew they would be interested in hearing about my excursion to the sugary, sandy beaches of the Caribbean, with its emerald green water and palm trees. Deep inside there was a battle brewing! How could I and would I tell them about this "mission trip" with forty preachers? How would I tell them that God called me to preach?

Rusty Cabiness was a special friend. His father was a superintendent at a textile mill. His mom was beautiful. I loved going to their house because they were "so cool." They had so much love for each other and really enjoyed life. I knew Rusty had a home life that I always wanted.

Rusty and I double-dated a lot, since I didn't have a car. I remember one occasion when Rusty dated Sissy Wilkins, and I dated Ann Goforth. The next weekend, we swapped. We were both crazy and enjoyed life in a small town.

Rusty, Johnny, and Jerry knew me too well. Wayne Brown saw only the church side of me, but playing football and going out on the weekends with Rusty, Johnny, and Jerry meant they saw me as I really was. Sad to say, I did not always "walk the walk" in high school.

Now I had turned the corner, come out of the closet, and was ready to go gung-ho for God. I really did not know how this would play with people who really knew me. However, I was now ready to take my stand for Christ, even if it meant I would stand alone!

"I can't do it! I'll just keep my mouth shut, graduate, and pursue ministerial studies afar off. I won't tell them!"

Just then, God reminded me of Romans 1:16, my new life verse. I must not be ashamed. I will tell them. There will be no reserves, no retreats, and no regrets.

When I got back to classes at BHS, Mr. Clary asked to me to share my experiences with the student body during our next student assembly. Every Friday, I presided over assembly at BHS. I was the president of the student body. My friend, Wayne Brown, was the president of our senior class.

Just as soon as Mr. Clary asked me to share, I received confirmation and affirmation from God. I knew the calling of God on my life. I knew that I had just made a crucial decision about the direction of my life. Now I had to communicate this to my friends. I didn't know how they might react, but that really didn't matter.

Next week in assembly, I tried to share what an awesome time I had with forty preachers. I knew some of my friends were choking with amusement. I told them about what God was doing in my life and what my Christian experience meant to me.

I knew some people thought "what a waste!" However, I was overwhelmed with the support I received from my friends. You see, all my friends were religious. They all had good Christian parents, and everyone went to church. They had no drug problem, no immorality, no alcohol. Occasionally, someone would sneak a beer, but I NEVER SAW ANY OF MY FRIENDS DRUNK! We were good but not godly! No one wanted to be known as a Christian fanatic. I was right in the middle and realized that I had not been a very good testimony.

God began to work in my life. He was also doing a wonderful work in others around me. Wayne Brown was spiritually strong. God would later call Wayne, and he surrendered to the ministry.

Suddenly, I had a heart for evangelism. I wanted to preach. I wanted to share my faith. I really wanted to see people around me come to know Christ.

Even with this desire, I found it hard to talk about Christ. Because I had been such a weak Christian in high school, I felt like a hypocrite sharing my faith.

I do remember one of the first people I led to Christ: my sister, Paula. Paula was a sweet girl. I always felt guilty around her because I left home in the ninth grade, while she stayed with my alcoholic parents. I knew it was a tough life for her. I knew she hated it as much as I did. Yet she stayed to help my two younger brothers, Eddie and Johnny.

My grandfather, Ernest Hardin, died after a stroke. Granddad was a hard-working man. He worked for years in a textile mill on the third shift. After working all night, he came home, changed clothes, and went out to plow or work in the cotton fields until about two in the afternoon. Then he would go to bed and sleep until it was time to go back to the mill.

He served as a trustee on the county school board and was a deacon at the First Baptist Church. He was quiet but well respected in the community.

I was still a teenager when he died. I remember driving the car to my parents' house. Paula was with me.

"Paula, do you know if you die that you will go to Heaven?" I asked.

"I'm not really sure," she said.

"Well, I will show you," I replied.

When we got to the house, I spoke with her and we prayed. Paula asked Jesus in her heart. We were both so happy. Little did I know that years later, Paula would marry a young preacher whose father was a great pastor of a large church in Columbus, Georgia. Nor did I know that they would give their lives to be foreign missionaries.

It was awesome to see her tears and hear her prayer. Paula had a genuine experience with Christ. I was happy to share God's love with her.

When I began to vocalize my desire to "get in the game" for God, I aroused the attention of Glen Isler. Glen was a consistent Christian who had a good testimony in our class. He carried his Bible, which I often saw him read in class. Glen prayed before he ate in the cafeteria. He went to Eastside Baptist Church, which was a lot more emotional than First Baptist Church. I liked Glen, but I didn't want to be with him. You see, Glen didn't play ball. He didn't have a girlfriend. He wasn't popular. He even went over to the Cherokee County jail in Gaffney every Sunday morning to preach to the inmates. I admired Glen "from a distance."

Then it happened.

Glen approached me and blurted out, "Ronnie, I am proud that you want to serve God. I'd like for you to go to jail on Sunday with me."

"Go to jail?" I thought. "Go with you? I don't think so. What would Rusty, Johnny, Jerry, and Wayne think? Why, they would think I had gone nuts!"

At that point, I realized how carnal I was. It was all about me! I cared what people thought. I worried what this new commitment was going to cost me! I had achieved stardom on the athletic field, become popular enough at school to be elected president of the student body, and set the pace for my future. And suddenly, I was worried about what people thought about my Christianity. That didn't make any sense.

"Sure!" I replied. "Can you come by and pick me up?"

My plan was to go to Gaffney, visit the jail with Glen, and get back home in time to go to Sunday school. No one had to know. And that is exactly what I did.

Glen came by and picked me up every Sunday. I would testify to the inmates and sometimes preach. I am sure people saw me with Glen, but I tried to hide it as much as possible. As much as I had admired Glen

45

from a distance, I just didn't want my friends to think I was a crazy, religious fanatic.

The time I spent with Glen was awesome! I learned the joy of serving Christ. I developed a boldness to speak up for Christ. I became balanced and unashamed to partner with people who chased God.

Meanwhile my friendship with Wayne, Rusty, Jane, Nancy, Jerry, and Kenneth Putnam grew stronger. I think the decisions I made concerning friends helped mold my values. I received positive reinforcement from my aunts and uncles, as well as all my cousins.

Being back home with my parents was a good decision. Mom and Dad were growing as Christians. They experienced such a change in their lives that you would never believe they ever drank alcohol. They lived in the Buffalo community and were active at Buffalo Baptist Church.

My strong commitment to Christ my senior year was a decision I would never regret. I only wish I had made the decision earlier. I still struggled spiritually. I really tried to live to please Christ despite my shortcomings and vulnerability to temptation. My goal was to go to Furman University and study for the ministry. However, there was a new pastor at Hopewell Baptist Church who really was a great preacher. Hopewell was where my uncle, E. J. Hardin, was a deacon. Many times I went with my cousin, Ernie, to hear Pastor Jesse Powers preach. His style was powerful, personal, and passionate. He used the Bible as the basis for his authority. I loved his zeal for lost sinners.

Rev. Powers had such an impact on me that I inquired to see if he went to Furman. Even though he was a Southern Baptist, I discovered that he went to school in Chattanooga, Tennessee. The name of the Bible College was Tennessee Temple College. I knew little of the school. All I knew was that I wanted to preach like Jesse Powers.

After I began making it known that God had called me to preach, my uncle, Jack Turney, wanted to talk to me. He told me that if I became a preacher, there was only one school for me to consider. My pastor told me that Furman was the place for me, so I expected Uncle Jack to confirm that. Jack said that I should attend a school that was fundamental and Bible-believing. Amazingly, Jack said that I should to go Tennessee Temple College.

Decisions, decisions! My pastor said Furman and Uncle Jack said Tennessee Temple. I was sure that I could get a scholarship to Furman. I won the conference mile run during my senior year, set a school record, and had a conversation with the Furman track coach, Chuck Rohle.

I planned a visit to Furman for a weekend. I went to Greenville to stay in the dorm and attend a couple of classes. Since Furman was a Southern Baptist institution, I figured everyone on campus was fired up for God. Boy, was I in for a shock. During my visit, I saw students drinking alcohol. I even saw a couple of football players turn a candy machine upside down to steal money. Knowing that I was not strong enough spiritually for such temptation, I ruled out Furman.

I was close to graduation but still couldn't decide. I considered Gardner–Webb College in Shelby, North Carolina. I was starting to get confused. Then Jack came by to see me again.

"Well, are you going to Tennessee Temple?" he asked.

"I don't know," I replied. "I don't know anyone there. I have never been to Chattanooga. I don't even know if I can get accepted."

"Oh, that's not a problem," Jack stated. "I'll call the vice president right now. I can get you accepted if you want to go to school there."

"Really? Well, call him," I answered.

I couldn't believe it when Jack was on the phone talking to the vice-president of the college. Dr. J.R. Faulkner was the vice-president, and Jack knew him personally.

"He said send your transcript, fill out an application, and they will make room for you," Jack stated.

This was amazing. God appeared to open this door. I was forced to make a decision. Little did I realize it at the time, but this decision was going to change my life, chart my future, and confirm my calling for my career.

Decisions really do determine your destiny! Going to Tennessee Temple was one of the most critical decisions of my life. I knew that this decision would color, shape, and impact God's calling on my life.

I had no margin for mistake in this decision. However, I was convinced that God in His sovereignty was leading me one step at a time. He gave me peace that this was the direction I needed to walk.

As an athlete, I knew decisions were so vital to winning. Later as a coach, I learned that decisions became critical as time elapsed. As we got closer to the end of the game, every decision was magnified. If you made a mistake, the game was lost. I actually lived for that moment! With adrenaline flowing and excitement high, I could control the outcome of the game by making the right calls. Right decisions put our team in a position to win!

As a teenager, I was making the right decisions. My destiny depended on it. With each decision, I was striving to win in the biggest game of all—life!

CHAPTER 5

WORKING

Working hard was always my legacy. I don't know why, but I have always walked faster, worked longer, and displayed a passionate personality in everything I did. No one EVER accused me of being "laid back." I was a type-A, let's-go-get-them, if-it's-to-be-then-it's-up-to-me, attack-hell-with-a-water-gun type guy.

One of the first places I went upon arriving in Chattanooga was the campus gymnasium. As an athlete, I was ready to get involved. I had turned down a track scholarship at Furman to come to Tennessee Temple, but I was ready to try out for the team. I was disillusioned to learn that they had no football or track. I excelled at these sports at Blacksburg. They did have basketball, but it was not my sport. Although I played on our high school team, we were terrible, thanks in part to my contribution.

However, as an athlete, I was ready to try out for the college basketball team. I knew I had a chance when I learned that the school had hired a new coach and only two players from the previous year were returning.

The coach was a young, new Christian and highly opinionated. It was truly his way or the highway. He was in charge and a strong leader. Actually, I liked him. As a Christian, Bruce Foster wanted everyone to be saved. His philosophy was to use basketball to preach the Gospel. His zeal for souls was the reason that he was fired from a high school in Colorado. He was preaching to all his players and trying to get them all born again. He brought that same passion to Tennessee Temple. I didn't know it then, but Bruce Foster would become a second dad to me—one of the most influential persons in my life.

I was afraid at the tryouts. We were all bad, but that helped my chances. There was only one problem—I was about the worst of the bad. As the three-day tryouts came to a close, my fate was uncertain.

"Boys, come by my office tomorrow," Coach instructed. "I will post the team on my door. If your name is on the list, you will report to practice on Monday."

With that announcement, he walked out of the gym. I just knew that I probably didn't have to worry about practicing on Monday. The next twenty-four hours were awful. I couldn't sleep. Did I make it? How could I really like this school if I was not on the team? I came from a high school where I won ten varsity letters, was the MVP of two sports, set a school record, and turned down a college scholarship. Now I had to wait to see if I made the team.

The next day, I ran to the gym at 3:00. The list was on the door.

With a name that starts with B, I looked at the top, but my name was not there. My heart sank. As I looked down the list, I realized that the list was not in alphabetical order.

"There it is!" I shouted. "There's my name—Bishop."

Yes, it was there, and it was the LAST name on the list. I didn't care because I was on the team!

"Bishop, come in here," Coach Foster demanded.

I walked in and Coach Foster told me to sit down. I was excited to be in the office of the head coach.

"Bishop, hustle makes up for lack of ability!" Coach said. "I'll see you on Monday."

I thought about the words—hustle makes up for lack of ability. Wow, what a powerful, trite statement. Later, it dawned on me. He was making a statement not TO me but ABOUT me. I was no good, so I had to hustle and work extremely hard to overcome my deficiencies.

Arriving at Tennessee Temple College was overwhelming. I really wasn't ready for this. First of all, there were so many people. When I enrolled as a freshman in 1963, there were 2,800 students in the student body, which was more people than lived in Blacksburg. Secondly, everyone dressed differently. These people seemed to be focused on serving God. They reminded me of my grandmother. Thirdly, the student handbook was filled with rules that scared me: no movies, no holding hands, no dating without chaperones. Why, they wouldn't let girls swim at the beach or swimming pool with boys. (They called it mixed bathing!) We had to cut our hair, go to church three times a week, attend chapel three times a week, and be in our room at 11:00 p.m., with lights out at 11:30.

Grandmother Hardin loved it, but I was scared and intimidated. As a freshman, I never dated a girl on campus. I waited until I went back to

Blacksburg. Nobody at home had ever heard of Tennessee Temple, so I knew it would be safe to "let my hair down."

Speaking of my grandmother, she had a vested interest in my studying for the ministry. You see, she had prayed for a preacher in the family. Her oldest son, Marvin, actually surrendered to preach and went to school to study for the ministry. However, he soon turned back and later died an alcoholic.

Grandmother had six sons, and none of the others were interested in ministry. So she gave up on the idea of a preacher in the family until I came along. Now her oldest grandson was destined to preach the Gospel.

Even though I lived in fear of breaking the rules of the school, I was determined to succeed in the ministry. I got involved from the very first day in evangelistic ministries. I went with friends to share at jails and the juvenile detention center.

"Ronnie, how would you like to preach?" a friend asked.

"You're kidding me? Of course!" I replied. "Where and when?"

"Next Saturday morning in downtown Chattanooga," he stated.

I contemplated about Saturday morning in downtown Chattanooga. The only church that met on Saturday morning was Seventh-day Adventist. Anyway, I planned to go. I was excited about preaching.

They picked me up that Saturday and downtown we went. I was puzzled when we stopped in front of the American National Bank. At 10 a.m. hundreds of people were on the streets.

"Here we are!" the leader exclaimed.

"Where's the church?" I asked.

"Church? We're here to preach to the lost," he countered.

"Where are they?"

"Ron, look, they are all over the streets," the group explained. "You stand right there on the corner and let her rip. Remember, quick three-minute sermon and keep it simple."

Well, I was in shock! There I was: a country boy from a small town standing on a corner in downtown Chattanooga preaching the Gospel to passersby. Think anybody cared? No one stopped to listen. No one introduced me. But I started shouting a sermon to the top of my lungs.

If my high school classmates had seen this, they would have flipped. I had to swallow a lot of pride. That street corner was humbling. Little did I realize it at the time, but faithfulness to obey the leadership of the Lord on that street corner would some day lead me to pulpits of some of the largest churches in America.

At Tennessee Temple I began to grow as a Christian. I decided to major in English and minor in Bible. I thoroughly enjoyed studying the Bible. I took Old Testament Survey and New Testament Survey during my freshman year. Later, I would study books of the Bible, ecclesiology, eschatology, and Greek. Perhaps the best class was personal evangelism. In this class, we studied how to lead a person to Christ.

The more I studied the Bible, the more I realized just how shallow and ignorant I was. Many of my friends were teens whose parents were teachers, deacons, or church workers. They had fathers who were pastors, evangelists, or famous missionaries. They knew the Bible and had been taught well. I felt a little intimidated by them.

"Ron, I saw you on campus with a new evangelical," my roommate, Dan Miller, stated. "And the other day I saw you with a Calvinist, a pseudo-fundamentalist, and a deeper-lifer."

I thought to myself, you've got to be kidding. Why are all these people on this campus?

"Well, Dan, I am confused," I said. "There seems to be so many groups on campus that I need to avoid. Back home in Blacksburg there were only two groups—saved and lost!"

Another thing I learned at Temple was that some on campus were not passionate about serving Christ; I know some had to be lost. They were a definite minority and not vocal at all. Their parents were in the ministry, and they had rebelled against God a long time. Sooner or later they were exposed, quit, or got expelled from school.

Meanwhile, I was growing more passionate about the Lord.

During my first month at Temple, I made a startling discovery! I found out that the school was not a Southern Baptist college. Someone told me that it was Independent Baptist. Now, I was raised in a Southern Baptist church. To be perfectly honest, I thought all Baptists were Southern Baptists. I didn't know there were Independent Baptists, Bible Baptists, Conservative Baptists, Regular Baptists, and Free-Will Baptists.

One day I walked by the bookstore and saw a book that captured my eyes: *Southern Baptists—Wake Up* by John R. Rice. I bought that book and began to read with interest. Dr. Rice spoke of all the liberalism, compromise, and denial of the essentials. He said that Southern Baptist seminary professors were denying the deity of Christ, the inspiration and inerrancy of the Scriptures, the blood atonement, and even the bodily resurrection of Christ. He went on to state that Cooperative–Program money, which was given to the local church, was supporting such seminaries and apostate teachers.

Suddenly, I felt that something needed to be done. I needed to tell my pastor and the people of First Baptist Church in Blacksburg. This church licensed Wayne Brown and me into the Gospel ministry. I knew we gave money to the Cooperative Program, the local association,

Lottie Moon, and Annie Armstrong. (I always wondered what these two women did with all the money we sent every year!)

Before Thanksgiving, I decided to make a trip home. Remember, I made the basketball team and the season was about to begin. That was my last chance to go home before Christmas.

Pastor Coy Miller called me and asked me to preach on Sunday night at FBC. Wow, this was awesome. I had been growing in my faith and studying the Bible. He wanted me to share with my home church. What would I say?

Southern Baptists, wake up!

The thought hit me, but how could I? This would not be a very popular subject. Some in our church didn't know if they were going to Heaven, but they did know they were Baptists!

With a lot of facts and quotes, I presented a very good and persuasive argument for why the Southern Baptists were drifting into liberalism. I had plenty of ammunition from Dr. Rice's book about many seminary professors who were, without a doubt, extremely liberal. I knew by firsthand experience that Furman and Wake Forest universities were hardly "Christian" schools.

Please understand that the people in Blacksburg loved me. First Baptist Church was where I was saved, baptized, and licensed to preach. The church gave me financial support, as they did all their ministerial students. However, this sermon stunned the people. They thought I had drifted into another denomination and was no longer Southern Baptist. Well, I still considered myself Southern Baptist, but I was at an Independent Baptist college.

In retrospect, I never should have preached this message, because it showed a lack of spiritual wisdom and discernment—I was just a novice. The result of this message was devastating to me. The church dropped my financial support. The Southern Baptists believed I was a traitor, and the Independent Baptists couldn't trust me. I found myself outside every camp.

I kept working hard! I wanted to be a good preacher. I wanted to travel, preach, and see souls saved. I felt God was leading me to be an itinerant evangelist. I studied and got involved in every opportunity to share Christ. My strategy to overcome obstacles and establish my identity in the Lord's work included diligent work and study, establishing relationships, and obligating myself to every invitation to minister.

CHAPTER 6

FINDING A TEAMMATE

Life at Tennessee Temple was good. Second only to my passion to study the Bible and preach was my love for basketball. It was through a piece of leather filled with air that I established my identity on campus, developed lasting friendships, and found a new avenue of ministry.

Our team was terrible the first year, but we were exciting to watch. We won only three games while losing twenty. However, since we played with such intensity, no one ever left our games. Coach Foster instilled in us a good work ethic and the belief that we could win every game. I learned to maximize my potential, which at the time was minimal to say the least.

I remember finally getting in a game my freshman year. I was a very nervous point guard. We were getting beat by thirty points with three minutes left to play. I was fouled on three consecutive trips down the floor. Talk about stupid! For someone with a huge lead to be fouling an opponent on three consecutive possessions is beyond reason.

As I stood on the free-throw line preparing to shoot, a teammate exclaimed, "C'mon, Ron we can still do it!"

Still do it? If we could still do it, my teammate and I would not be in the game. If we could still do it, we would still be on the bench.

I hit six free throws that night and had six points in three minutes. My roommates told me that Coach Foster was crazy for not playing me more.

"With six points in three minutes, you'd average forty points a game like Bobby Murr," they said. I knew right then that friends, family, girlfriends, and roommates did not have a clue about the game.

Still, I was meeting teammates who would become lifelong friends. Joe Jordan was also from a dysfunctional home with an alcoholic and abusive father. We talked a lot on road trips about our home life. Both of us had a strong desire to make our lives count for God. Joe was a great shooter with tremendous range. He had been saved at Word of Life Island in New York. Later, he would travel to Argentina with his wife, Melva, and build a great Word of Life ministry, training thousands of Hispanics to serve Christ. Presently, Joe is the executive director of Word of Life International, on which I serve as a member of the board of directors.

Dan Sherman was about ten years older than the rest of the team. Dan was about 6'4" tall, and he also had a passion to share the Gospel. He became a pastor and served several churches. Dan has remained a strong Christian and has been like an older brother to me.

Randy Faulkner, Rick Calenburg, Dan Manley, Paul Martin, and Richard Pankey were other teammates who later served Christ in special ways as pastors, teachers, and missionaries. Bobby Hodges, Bobby Murr,

Steve Fazekas, Jerry Day, and others were involved in business but were faithful to church work.

Surrounded by such spiritual teammates, I found great balance as a Christian athlete. These relationships helped me understand how I could use sports as a ministry. Coach Foster taught us that soul-winning was the essential way to serve the Lord. Therefore, every road trip became an opportunity to win the lost. Often, as we traveled through north Alabama or the mountains of north Georgia, we got lost. However, passing through many small towns gave us an opportunity to "hit the streets," to pass out Gospel tracts, and to engage in confrontational witnessing.

Coming from a small town myself, I realize how intimidating it must have been to have this tall group of athletes come out of nowhere to declare people "going to hell" if they didn't get saved.

Although we didn't win many games, we came back to campus with many professions of faith as the result of our aggressive evangelizing. Looking back, I am so indebted to Coach Foster for teaching me to love the lost. I owe a debt to him for allowing God to use him to burn a passion in my heart for the souls of men.

My career as a college basketball player was not bad. Remember, I started out as the last one selected from the tryouts. However, a year later, I won a scholarship. By the end of my sophomore year, a starter was bitten by the love bug, and I got more playing time.

Then it happened! I became the starting point guard my junior year. Playing along with Bobby Murr, we established a record number of victories. Bobby led the nation in scoring with an average of forty points-per-game. He was phenomenal. Although we did not keep good stats on assists, I figured I led the nation in assists. Everyone on our team was keenly aware that if Bobby didn't get forty to fifty points in a game, then our chances of winning were slim. I averaged fourteen points, but only because the man guarding me was helping guard Bobby.

God used Bobby in a special way. After graduation he surrendered to be an evangelist with Word of Life. Later, he became a pastor. After serving Christ for many years, Bobby had a moral failure in his life. The result was that he lost his family. One of the greatest things Bobby ever did was to father five precious boys and a daughter. Bobby remarried and became a very successful business man, but he never finished his role in the ministry. Tim, David, Joel, Andy, and Steve are all phenomenal people. Tim and Joel are preachers and work in a Christian school. David and Steve coach in Christian high schools. Andy is a policeman in North Carolina. They all followed their dad's steps by becoming great basketball players at Tennessee Temple University. These boys deserve a lot of credit, but their success should be attributed to their mom, Susie.

After Bobby graduated, it was my time to step forward on the basketball team. Coach Foster named me one of the captains. We had a great year, and I was named to the Southern Christian Athletic Conference All-Star team. Wow, what a turnaround! We went from 3–20 my first year to a 22–8 record my senior year. More amazing was the fact that I went from the last person selected in tryouts to becoming the captain four years later. I made the all-conference team and averaged fifteen points per game.

My basketball success became possible only through hard work, focus, and determination. I also believe that God was working out His plan for my life. I was beginning to realize how sports would play a huge role in my passion to serve Christ.

Following the end of my career in 1967, two monumental things happened to me. In May 1967, I graduated with a Bachelor of Arts degree; and in August, I married Patricia Ann Reagan.

Girls had been a big part of my life since my sophomore year in high school. I dated Sissy Wilkins, Ann Goforth, and Nancy Wilson. I was in love with Nancy, but knowing I would go away to college meant an end of our relationship was near.

In college I did not date anyone for a year. The transition to a Christian college with all the rules intimidated me. The school forbade holding hands and kissing, and even had a rule that you must stay six inches away from the opposite sex. I mean, there was no personal contact. The chaperone thing was ridiculous to me. Therefore, I determined not to date anyone until I got adjusted to the school. To put it simply, I did not trust myself and was fearful of being expelled.

During my sophomore year I fell in love with a beautiful girl from Fayetteville, North Carolina. Jo Phyllis Thompson was Miss Fayetteville her senior year in high school. She had a tremendous personality and desire to serve Christ. When her parents discerned that we were getting too serious, they withdrew her from TTU and sent her to Bob Jones University. Though the feelings were very strong, that relationship soon diminished with time and distance.

I also dated other girls such as Nancy Walker and Brenda Bryant. Nancy was the niece of Coach Foster, and I probably dated her to please Coach. Both girls were cheerleaders at TTU.

During the summer of 1966, I went to Word of Life Island in the Adirondack Mountains in upstate New York. There, on a beautiful island in the middle of Schroon Lake, I served as athletic director at one of the largest youth camps in America. I spent ten weeks at WOL. Although I worked hard using sports to impact thousands of teenagers, God was working in a very significant way in my life. Friends such as M. A. Butler, Joe Jordan, and Don Kelso were encouraging me in my walk with the Lord. Weekly campfires on the island, where teens were challenged to throw a stick on the fire to represent the full commitment of their life to do the will of God, made a huge impression on me. Even though I had committed to serving Christ, one night I went forward at a campfire with the campers. I threw a stick on the fire and pledged to God that I was placing my life on His altar to burn out for Him. That was one of the most significant moments of my life.

When I arrived back at TTU in September, I was about to be swept off my feet. It all started so innocently. As the new students arrived on campus to begin their freshman year, I was suddenly feeling the pride of being one of the big men on campus. This was my senior year.

I went to the Happy Corner, which was the snack shop on campus. There I saw the most beautiful girl I had ever seen. She had a dark complexion. I figured she had been out in the sun a lot. That beautiful tan was also accented by the fact that she was a Cherokee Indian descendant. I found out her name was Patricia Reagan from Atlanta. I remember she wore an A-line navy skirt with white blouse, red coat, and navy knee socks. This was a freshman that I had to meet.

As I stood at the counter of the Happy Corner next to her, I noticed a ring. Suddenly, I was devastated! Later, through her roommate, I learned that she came to TTU with some friends from Brookwood Baptist Church. Pat had surrendered to missions at her home church during a missions conference with Rev. Mel Rutter. Even though she was a freshman and I was a senior, I learned she was only one year younger than me. After graduating from Roosevelt High School in Atlanta, she went to work for the Federal Reserve Bank.

"She's engaged?" I asked. "To whom?"

"To a guy back in Atlanta," replied her friend.

As I walked away, I thought, so the guy's back in Atlanta. Well, she is not married, so being engaged doesn't matter to me. I felt so much self-confidence that I was ready to make a move. After all, I was the star athlete and a BMOC!

Naturally, the inquiries I was making about this beautiful girl were getting back to her. We began to watch each other on campus, in the dining hall, in Chapel, and in the Happy Corner. Our eyes met a lot, and there were smiles. However, weeks passed before I could get the courage to talk to her. I was a little shy, even though cocky.

Finally, one day I saw her on campus and struck up a conversation. I was too nervous to remember what was said. I do remember that she was no longer wearing the ring. She had broken off the engagement with the guy back in Atlanta. Now I was free to make a move. That's all I talked about in the dorm. However, weeks turned to months, and I still had not asked her for a date.

Christmas vacation was nearing. Pat had come to McGilvray Gymnasium several times with her roommates to see me play basketball. I always looked for her in the stands. Just before the holiday break, our music department always put on Handel's *Messiah*. This was my chance. So in December 1966, I mustered up the courage, called Pat, and asked her to go with me to the *Messiah*. I was in a daze when she said yes!

When I picked her up at the dorm, the magic continued to cast its spell on me. She was wearing a new white dress. She was so petite, so beautiful, so tanned. The music was great, but the chords being played in my heart were pulsating.

I took her home on Christmas and met her parents. They could tell we were in love, but they were not impressed. Our relationship grew over the following months. I wanted to marry her, but I didn't know how she would feel being married to an evangelist. We talked about it. We would live by faith. I would be gone a lot. I wanted her so badly. I was relieved to know that she was willing to walk beside me and serve Christ with me for the rest of our lives.

Eight months after our first date, Pat and I were married at Brookwood Baptist Church in Atlanta on August 12, 1967. Her pastor and Coach Foster performed the ceremony. Besides being saved, this was the greatest day of my life. I now had a lover, a helpmeet, and a friend who would journey with me through life as we walked by faith to serve our Lord together.

I could see the hand of God working to prepare us for each other. I knew that Pat had many choices, but God had miraculously brought her into my life. I can honestly say that she possessed all the qualities that I needed to make me complete. I also could have gone other directions; however, I knew that I would never have been happy or able to effectively serve God in His will without Pat!

As a coach, I made a lot of decisions. My success depended upon making right decisions. One bad decision in a critical moment of the game could bring defeat. In life, a person is also faced with decisions. Accepting Christ at the age of nine and marrying Pat were the two greatest decisions I ever made. Those two decisions made me a WINNER in the bigger game of life.

EXECUTING GOD'S PLAYBOOK

CHAPTER 7

EARLY MINISTRY

After graduation from college, I entered seminary and simultaneously began my coaching career. My desire was to earn the Master of Divinity degree. Tennessee Temple had a seminary, so it was natural for me to stay at TTU. My bride could also work on finishing her degree.

Coach Foster asked me to be his graduate assistant basketball coach. So at the young age of twenty–one, I launched into a career of college coaching. Coach Foster was the athletic director, and he named me the head baseball and soccer coaches. I NEVER PLAYED EITHER SPORT. If you know Coach Foster, this was not optional or something to pray about. So I became a coach, which helped me pay for seminary.

I never had seen a soccer game! In fact, the first game I ever saw was my debut as the coach. My competitive juices, my athletic savvy, and my ability to judge and recruit talent were distinguishing traits. A Christian college campus has a lot of international students and missionary kids, raised in foreign countries. Therefore, I appealed to the student body and found a lot of interest from these people who grew up in countries where soccer was the only sport.

Having Pat Freeney, a missionary kid who was a little older than most college guys, and Larry Rosser made the job easy. Larry was raised by missionary parents in Nicaragua. He could handle the ball and kick it with unstoppable power. These two, plus a goalie named Terry Taggart, formed the nucleus of our new team. I put a few other foreign players on the front line to score. As for all the Americans, who, like me, didn't know what was going on but loved contact, I put them back on the defense. Our motto became "bust 'em and boom the ball."

I became like the hero on campus who originated this new team sport and coached it to a 6–5 record in its inaugural year. Five years later, we won 16 and lost 3 and were state champs. We beat the University of Kentucky, University of Tennessee, University of Georgia, and Vanderbilt. I was named by sportswriters as the collegiate soccer "Coach of the Year" in Tennessee—not bad for a guy who was 26 years old, never played the sport, and never saw a game before coaching one.

This only confirmed the fact that I was born to coach. God had gifted me with the attributes needed to put a team together and win games.

I wish I could report that my baseball career was as successful. I coached baseball for only three years. My record was right at .500. Still, I was not ashamed since I never played baseball in high school or college. How many college coaches do you know who never played on a competitive team in the sport they coached? Again, I was unique and gifted by God.

However, basketball was the king of sports to me. I loved coaching with Coach Foster. Being his assistant meant that I sat next to him, kept some stats, handed him the chalkboard, and kept my mouth shut.

I don't ever remember Coach Foster asking me for advice. I handled details and patted the players on the back after Coach had kicked their butt.

I watched, listened, and learned. At the time, I never knew that God was preparing me for the day when I would be a college basketball head coach.

During my time in seminary, I was learning Greek and Hebrew. I studied ecclesiology, eschatology, and evangelism. Pat was working at a medical clinic and taking a full load of courses. The studies, our marriage, and my coaching career kept our plates full. However, Pat and I were busy serving the Lord. Because I was a former college player and currently a college coach, I began to receive a lot of invitations to speak in churches. I never turned down an invitation to speak at a youth rally or a Sunday service. I never considered myself a coach who happened to preach but a preacher who happened to coach. For me, athletics was the platform to share the Gospel of Christ.

Balancing time with my wife, studies in seminary, and coaching became a challenge for me. Keep in mind that I was a young married man who was a senior on the college team the year before. One year later, I was a coach who lived a block off campus in an apartment that Pat and I rented for $55 a month. Players from the basketball team came over at all hours of the night. Many times we fed them the last food we had in the house.

After the first year, I took the position as youth pastor at Unity Baptist Church. It was my first position on a church staff. I also enrolled at Middle Tennessee State University to work on my master's degree in physical education.

Can you believe that? I was going to seminary, going to graduate school, coaching, and working as a youth pastor—all at the same time! I have always been busy working and a little crazy at times.

Pastor Billy Joe Smith and the deacons at Unity thought I should be ordained. In 1970, I was ordained into the Gospel ministry at Unity. Evangelist Bill Stafford preached my ordination, and several of my seminary professors served on the ordination council.

Pat worked hard to finish her degree in elementary education, while working a full-time job to help our finances at home. She is also a passionate, focused person, driven to excellence. She was my best friend and encouraged me to persevere through all the pressures I faced. Pat was also an excellent mentor to teenage girls and provided great spiritual assistance in my ministry at Unity Baptist.

In 1971 after three years of marriage, Pat became pregnant. I was so thrilled! I was going to be a father. We had bought a small house. (It was so exciting preparing for a new child.) I thought Pat was beautiful as she began to show her pregnancy. We bought baby furniture and prepared for the arrival of our first little one.

October 25, 1971, was another monumental and happy day for me. I took Pat to Memorial Hospital in Chattanooga. All I remember was how nervous I was. I always thought myself to be cool, and I coached with little nervousness. However, I was so nervous that I was silly. I am so glad my mother-in-law had come from Atlanta. At approximately 1:30 p.m., Robyn Michelle arrived.

My first sight of Robyn was amazing. This little girl, who weighed 8 pounds, 8 ounces, had a full head of hair. She was beautiful. She was perfect. She was mine. Pat suffered to give birth to a precious little girl, and suddenly our lives were changed. I was now Evangelist Ron Bishop, Coach Ron Bishop, and "Daddy."

Robyn brought so much joy to our home. She was always "my little lady." Pat always dressed her as a distinctively beautiful little girl. Her demeanor was so pleasant. I could never fully describe how proud Robyn made me feel.

During my fourth year of coaching, a church in Alabama called me to preach both Sunday services. I had been to Morgan County several times to preach in youth rallies. I knew the area and people well. Wyman Logan had recommended me to Bethel Baptist Church.

I found out that Bethel had been led out of the Southern Baptist Convention by a pastor who later resigned to pastor another Southern Baptist church. I thought that was a little strange! But the church brought in its first Independent Baptist pastor, who almost destroyed what was left. I guess he was typical for the late 1960s. He was legalistic, arbitrary, mean, and definitely independent. After months of being wounded from the pulpit, the deacons asked him to leave.

I looked at that audience on that Sunday. I was only 26-years-old but discerned that these people needed to feel the joy and warmth of a real relationship with Christ. I encouraged them in the Lord. It must have been good, because they asked me to come back the next week.

The trip was 140 miles from Chattanooga to Hartselle, Alabama, on a two-lane, dangerous highway. Pat didn't go with me because she stayed home with our first child.

After two weekends, the chairman of deacons, Brother Larrimore, asked me if I would consider being their pastor. Of course I said no! Finally, they asked if I would consider being an interim pastor. I could still coach and the second income would be helpful with our new child. This had some merit, even to a guy whose goal was to be an evangelist. If I accepted, it would mean traveling 280 miles round trip. All of my weekends would be focused on Bethel Baptist Church, until they found a pastor.

After prayer, Pat and I felt this was the direction God was pointing. So I called and committed to pastor the church on an interim basis. Well, God began to bless the ministry. The church began to grow. People were being saved. The offerings increased, and the pulpit committee stopped looking.

"Ron, we really believe you are our man," Frank Sharrott, a deacon, stated to me.

"I can't be! I plan on being an evangelist, Frank," I replied.

Besides, after six months, I was getting tired of that long trip. Some weekends I rode the Greyhound bus to Huntsville, where another deacon named Carlos Goodwin would meet me. He usually loaned me his red Firebird for the weekend. I was one cool, young pastor.

During the entire time, God was working in my life. But was I ready to give up my coaching career? Was I ready to leave the city life of Chattanooga to take my darling wife and beautiful baby daughter to a country town of only eight-thousand people?

I wrestled with the decision. Finally, I met with Frank Sharrott and told him I would make myself available to pastor Bethel Baptist Church. He was excited. Two weeks later, the church voted on me and I got almost a 100 percent vote. One family voted against me, but I was assured by Frank that they would always vote against everything. They were staunch Southern Baptists, determined to save their church. He was right! We always had three dissenting votes at every business meeting.

The church began to grow. We went from 123 to more than 250 people in a short period of time. Our giving doubled and our missions giving increased 15 percent. I was baptizing about ten people a month. The church suddenly had new life and once again felt a sense of pride in the community. That seemed to be my mission in pastoring Bethel Baptist. The church was hurting before I became pastor. People in the community felt the church had been stolen. It didn't help that a remnant went less than a mile down the road to start another church.

As a young pastor, I focused on the young people—singles and young married couples. I got involved in the community and joined the ministerial association. (I was the only Independent Baptist in that group.) I preached at a combined community Thanksgiving service at the First Baptist Church. Our entire church participated.

Our people began to feel good about their church. They went to work, and our impact was felt by the community. People came to see what was happening. God was healing His people, and the church was marching forward. We launched a building program to provide more space for the crowds that began to show up. The revivals in our church had an effect on the entire town. Promotion has always been a gift for me. I got nationally known speakers and brought them to our little church. I rented billboards on the highways to promote our meetings. I developed a great relationship with the publisher of our town newspaper. Coverage of our revivals and crowds was extensive. Some of our special events doubled our regular attendance. God honored us with His presence— that's the main thing.

We were so happy in Hartselle. It was a lot like Blacksburg to me, though it was a little larger. It had six traffic lights instead of one. Pat and I loved Bethel. I did my first baptism at Bethel. I also conducted my first wedding and funeral there. I was so nervous at the wedding, probably more than the bride or groom. All I remembered was I dismissed the audience before the mothers marched out.

We lived in a parsonage across the street. I fondly remember taking Robyn by the hand and walking her across the street to church. I also remember putting a University of Tennessee sweatshirt on her and putting her picture in the *Hartselle Enquirer* on her second birthday. Needless to say, we found out quickly that Alabama football, including Auburn and the University of Alabama, was itself a state religion. They hated Tennessee. Coach Bear Bryant was an alternate member of the Trinity.

To relate to the people, we had our first garden. One of our men raised chickens, and I got three loads of chicken litter in a borrowed pickup truck. I burned the garden up twice, but the extra I threw in the yard meant I needed a bush hog to cut my grass one month later. The ladies of the church laughed so hard when they heard that Pat didn't know that turnips actually grew in the ground under the turnip greens. I even helped the teens toilet paper a deacon's house.

Pat became pregnant again. The church was so excited. Most of their pastors in the past were like Sarah and Abraham—too old to have children. They got excited that a new church baby would be born and live in their parsonage.

On November 14, 1974, Rhonda Lynn was born at Decatur General Hospital, ten miles from Hartselle. This girl was so special. She had a beautiful, dark complexion like Pat and a face that even today is so beautiful. Who cares that she didn't have any hair? The hair that later grew was dark, and she looked like a little doll.

Our friends, Frank and Margaret Sharrott, became like grandparents to Robyn and Rhonda. This arrangement worked out well since our parents were so far away and the Sharrotts never had children.

It is amazing how close I became to Frank. I was always taught that a pastor should not become too close to a deacon. At my age, I couldn't help it. I leaned on Frank for wisdom and direction. Unlike many aspiring young ministers today, I was keenly aware of the fact that

I did not know everything. I had experience preaching and was well-educated, but pastoring a church was an awesome task, and I needed guidance. I wish every young evangelist and missionary would pastor a church in the USA for at least three years to develop an understanding of the local church. Nothing substitutes for that experience. It certainly cannot be learned in a seminary textbook

After 40 years of ministry, which includes traveling and preaching in twenty–five countries, founding a world-wide ministry, and being known in Baptist circles all over America, I can truthfully say that my tenure at Bethel was the most fulfilling, rewarding, and significant work I ever did. That ministry probably had the longest-lasting impact on me and my family. Our experiences at Bethel Baptist Church, especially the relationships and ministry of those good people, continue to impact us today.

CHAPTER 8

COACHING

The phone rang. E. C. Haskell, a friend who was director of admissions at Tennessee Temple College, was on the line.

"Ron, got some news for you," he said. "Bruce Foster just resigned as athletic director and head basketball coach."

"What?" I asked. "What's that all about?"

"Well, he's going into evangelism," E. C. stated. "But listen, would you be interested in the job?"

That question was more stunning than hearing my coach had resigned.

"Look," E. C. continued. "We just came out of a board meeting and I mentioned your name as a possible replacement, but Dr. Roberson said he did not think you would consider it since your church is doing so well. The job would be yours with no search if you want it."

Wow, this was a shock. Would I leave Bethel Baptist after three years of fantastic ministry to go back into coaching? What would Pat think about this?

"E. C., you tell Dr. Roberson I am interested," I said. "I need 24 hours to talk with Pat and consider, but call me back tomorrow."

I knew this was going to be another one of those monumental decisions in life. All my life I wanted to be an evangelist, but I needed a platform to launch into evangelism. I could not possibly leave the ministry to coach unless the priority would be to use athletics as a means to an end.

During my initial coaching years, I was invited to go with Sports and Cultural Exchange to coach a soccer team on a sports missions trip to Mexico. I told the founder and president, Jim Gordon, that I was not a very good soccer strategist. Jim knew of my success with an outstanding record and coach-of-the-year honors.

"Look we want you to go, Ron," Jim exclaimed. "You don't have to be a good coach. The players we selected are All-Americans. All you have to do is manage them, substitute, and give a halftime speech."

Now I may have been a novice soccer coach, but I could give those halftime speeches. I knew that God gifted me in the area of exhortation, encouragement, and kicking an athlete's tail if needed.

On that trip to Mexico, I saw how a coach could do two things. I experienced how you could use a sport to present the Gospel to thousands of spectators. I also saw how a coach could use sports to mentor and impact individual athletes.

Yes, I was interested in the job. In my heart, I knew this would advance my goals to preach to multitudes. This was my calling. Basketball would become the vehicle.

I knew I had to present this to Pat. I also had to inform my deacons and the church. Last of all, I had to justify my motives to my friends. I did not want anyone to think that I was leaving the ministry. I was convinced that I would be on a fast track, gain national recognition, and establish the relationships that would help me achieve my ultimate and eternal goals.

The call from E. C. came on Friday. I immediately discussed the idea with Pat. The invitation to coach flattered both of us. We knew this would devastate our church, but we also believed this was the plan of God and the next step we had to make.

Very few people have the opportunity to become a college head basketball coach. I would never be able to justify this move without making a career in coaching a platform for ministry.

Late that evening, I called E. C. back.

"E. C., I'm going to take the job," I stated. "However, it must be done right. I want to present my resignation and explanation to my church on Sunday."

My decision was supposed to be on top of the agenda for the faculty board meeting Saturday morning. E. C. had presented me with the schedule of announcing my hiring in the Sunday morning edition of the Chattanooga newspaper. At the time, two newspapers competed in Chattanooga: *The Chattanooga Times*, which was a morning newspaper, and *The Chattanooga News-Free Press*, an afternoon newspaper. They were fierce competitors, but The Chattanooga Times did not have a Sunday edition. The plan was to break the news on Sunday morning, so that I could announce my resignation in Hartselle in the Sunday morning service.

Late on Friday night I got a call from Jack Hodges, sportswriter for *The Chattanooga Times*.

"Ron, I understand you have been offered and accepted the position of athletic director and head basketball coach at Temple. Is that correct?" Jack asked.

A cold sweat broke across my brow. Would I deny the story or tell Jack Hodges the truth?

"Jack, I have been offered the job and I will accept it tomorrow morning," I stated. "I'll be in Chattanooga in the morning for a news conference."

"Well, you know we don't have a Sunday edition, so I'm going to break the story in our Saturday morning paper," he said.

"Jack, you can't do that!" I stated emphatically.

"Why not?" he quizzed.

"Well, I must first tell my church and explain it to them," I explained. "I don't want anyone in this town to know about this until I speak to my friends here in Hartselle. This town and my church have been good to me, and I refuse to treat them with a lack of respect."

"You've confirmed my story, Ron," Jack said. "So I must write the story."

"Jack, you do what you think you must do as a professional. However, if you write the story for your Saturday morning edition before it is officially announced by the university and before I resign my church position, I will not accept the job," I said with strong conviction. "You will have egg on your face, but I must do what is right!"

I could tell by the silence that Jack had been trumped. But I knew as a young man that I had to do what was right even if it cost me my dream job.

"OK," Jack said. "Well, good luck. We look forward to working with you. I hope you will give us the break on any staff changes or announcements on recruits."

"You got it, Jack," I closed. "And thanks for your professionalism in allowing me to do what I feel is right."

As a 29 year old man, I knew I had been tested to do right, even if it cost me a great opportunity in the ministry. It is called being ethical, and I had just passed the test.

However, I now faced another huge hurdle. I had to resign my church, and I knew it would be very hard to hurt the people who had become my family.

No one in my church suspected what was coming, except my buddy, Frank Sharrott. He was like a father to me and I wanted to prepare him. He tried to talk me out of it but came to the conclusion that I was leaving. I remember preaching to a full house that Sunday. I preached hard. I gave the invitation for people to come forward and several responded.

The time had come! I told the church there was a matter of business that had to be addressed. With a lot of emotion, I announced my resignation. Suddenly, the mood became like a funeral. People were crying; Pat and I were crying. I knew a lot of people were hurt.

"You can't do this, Brother Ron," Lucille Hall said. "What will we do?"

Lucille and Millard were special to me. She was the most active woman in our church. Millard was in charge of church grounds. Even though he did not have to do so, he cut my grass every week. Here was a man literally old enough to be my father who loved me and humbly served "his pastor." Their daughter, Deborah, was one of our most active teenagers. She studied the Bible, attended all youth functions, and master-minded the toilet paper raid on our parsonage. The Halls were like family, and I knew they were hurting on this Sunday.

After a lot of hugs and tears, I walked out of the building. I felt bad. I knew it was God's will, but I would have gladly stayed in Hartselle, Alabama until I died.

All afternoon I received calls. People in our church called. Friends at Tennessee Temple called. People who lived across America also called to offer congratulations.

I preached at Bethel Baptist Church for several weeks after the resignation. I wanted to help them. I didn't want to just walk out without some notice. During this time, I found a lot of reasons to cry. This was a very difficult time for all of us.

After weeks of finishing my responsibilities, it was time to move. Frank Sharrott had come to help me move from Chattanooga to Hartselle, but he told me he would not help me move back. I knew he was hurt. He cared for me and loved Pat and the girls.

Little did I know that he would become my closest friend. Frank and Margaret attended both our daughters' weddings and sat as their grandparents. We will visit them and talk to them regularly, because they will always be family to us.

CHAPTER 9

BACK TO CHATTANOOGA

S ince I was a teenager I have always felt like a champion. It seems like everything I did made me a winner. Sam Woolwine, a sportswriter with the *Chattanooga News Free Press*, wrote an article about me. The story was about how I was a winner in everything I did. I must confess that God has been good to me.

As a high school athlete, I was the MVP in track for four years and never lost a conference mile run. In football, I was quarterback, captain, and MVP on a championship team. Eventually, I was named to my high school sports Hall of Fame. Academically, I was an honor student and president of the student body.

In college, I became a two-time all-conference basketball player. I was MVP on my college team during my senior year and led the team to a 22–8 record. I was captain of the team. In college, I was vice-president of the student body.

However, when I left Hartselle and moved to Chattanooga to become athletic director and head basketball coach, I never could have imagined what would follow. I eventually found myself in the National Christian College Athletic Association Hall of Fame, Chattanooga Sports Hall of Fame, and the Tennessee Temple University Hall of Fame. Twice, I would be named the NCCAA National Coach of the Year.

God was good to me. I can only declare His glory, because I remember where I came from. My dad was not a preacher, a deacon, or even a Sunday school teacher! My mother was not a Sunday school teacher. I came from a dysfunctional home in a small town of two-thousand people with only one red light. I did not go to a conservative church with a pastor preaching expository messages from the Word of God. I never attended a Christian school until college. I even left home in the ninth grade.

I had no advantages at all. I was probably the least likely to succeed in my Christian life. Most everyone in the ministry today can attribute their success to their Christian parents, fundamental teaching of the Bible, conservative church life, and a pastor who mentored them in spiritual things. However, I was totally unexplainable. Only God could find me, call me, equip me, encourage me, and engage me in His work. The ONLY way you can explain my success is God.

I never felt that I pulled myself up by the boot straps, that I knew someone special, or that I was in the right place at the right time. I am a winner only because I met Christ. I am a champion only because I died to my game plan and followed His plan. He is sovereign, and His sovereign plan for my life made me who I am and what I am!

Moving back to Chattanooga was part of that plan. Pat and I could even see the hand of God in finding a house. While I was serving my notice as pastor, we drove to Chattanooga to find a house. Several friends lived in Ross Hills in Ringgold, Georgia. E. C. Haskell, my friend who helped me get the Temple job, lived on Richard Drive, about twelve miles from campus. He and several Temple faculty lived in Ross Hills.

We saw a house on Richard Drive that was new and available. It was a nice split-foyer house with about two-thousand square feet. Pat and I liked the house. We found out that the house was built by Rev. Billy Joe Smith. I couldn't believe it! Billy Joe was the pastor at Unity Baptist Church, where I was hired as youth pastor. Billy Joe was the pastor of the church where I was ordained. Now he had this beautiful house that had been sitting idle for nine months after being constructed.

When I called Billy Joe, he was happy that I was coming back to the Chattanooga area. When I asked about the house, he confirmed that it was for sale and that we could look at it.

"Well, what do you think?" Billy Joe asked.

"Wow, we like it," I said. "But how much do you want for it?"

"The market is slow right now and we've had to pay interest on it for nine months," he explained. "Ron, I'll let you have it for $36,000."

I was stunned. I thought, how could I afford a $36,000 house? Could I get a loan? I had a little money but not much.

"Well I'll have to go to a bank and see if I can get a loan," I replied. I knew that the chairman of the board of directors at Tennessee Temple University was the president of First Federal Bank in Chattanooga.

It soon became apparent to me that being named the athletic director and head basketball coach at Tennessee Temple University carried a lot of weight. The university had a great reputation in Chattanooga, and most of the city officials, bankers, educators, lawyers, and other professionals look on the university approvingly. Besides, I had great credit ratings. I even had several options available to me to get the needed funds to purchase the house.

I never made a counter offer. I believed Billy Joe had given me a good price, so we shook hands and had a deal.

This transaction was an affirmation to me that God was at work on my behalf. I knew that in spite of the difficulty of the decision, I was right where God was moving! Whether it is a job, a house, a game, or whatever, I must declare the wonderful works of God. Everyone knows it isn't about me!

Landing a house was my first priority. Now I had to turn my attention to my new profession. I knew that to build a championship program, I needed to put two things in place quickly. One was a staff and the other was player personnel.

Keep in mind that I entered this job with only one thing in mind—success. I wanted to win and win fast. Even though I was one of the youngest head coaches in the nation at the college level, I didn't leave a successful church ministry to finish second or third! Winning and capturing championships was my goal. By being successful as a college coach, I could establish myself on a platform that would impact people with the Gospel.

My first objective was to hire DeWayne Glascock as my assistant coach. "Lefty" was on Coach Foster's staff. He played for TTU when I was an assistant. Coach Foster had recruited a great incoming freshman class, and I knew we had to keep those ponies in our stable.

"Lefty, this is Ron," I said. "I need you to stay on board our coaching staff. You will be my assistant. I need you to contact our players and make sure they arrive on campus soon."

"I am happy for you and I'm honored you want me," Lefty said. "I'll begin calling all the players today. I've been talking to them, so I believe they are all committed to play for us."

Lefty was a knowledgeable coach with a lot of energy. He did not care about the limelight. He did not have great people skills, but he understood the game and could break it down, analyze, and teach players how to play. He was a defensive genius and could get players to excel on the end of the court where little glory was to be had.

Most importantly, Lefty had one quality that few young coaches, preachers, missionaries, or businessmen possess. He was loyal! I believe loyalty to authority and to one's superiors demonstrates character, humility, and a sense of servanthood.

After Lefty committed to assist me, we immediately began to call our players. What a group of great guys: Jerry Adams, Mitch Steiner, Jim Hubbard, Tony Phelps, and Jim Shoemate. These guys, paired with veteran teammates, 6'7" sharp shooter Victor Hazard and All-American Dan Smith, formed the foundation of a future national championship team.

Our first year was like a dream. At the conclusion of the season, I turned 30 years old. To be so young and have one year of head-coaching experience was encouraging. Although we had struggles during the season with two of our players, the team concluded the season with a17–12 record. Even though I felt good about it, the record would end up being the worst of my 10 year career.

I did not know what would follow. I did know how to work hard. I began to establish a network of relationships across America to build a national base of recruiting. To build our summer sports camps program, I spent time writing and calling Christian high school coaches throughout the Southeast and Midwest. I wrote to five-thousand pastors, introducing myself and telling them that I had ten full athletic scholarships available to superior Christian athletes who excelled in basketball.

The work paid off! From the very beginning, we developed the largest sports camps in the USA. One summer we put on a special week that attracted seven-hundred campers and three-hundred coaches. We offered athletes instruction in four sports and conducted clinics and seminars for the coaches. I brought in coaches from the University of Alabama, Tennessee, and Vanderbilt to be special speakers. We threw a banquet for the coaches and brought in nationally known speakers, such as Bobby Richardson, baseball Hall-of-Famer with the New York Yankees, and Pat Williams, general manager and vice-president of the NBA Philadelphia 76ers.

The letters to five-thousand pastors gave me a lot of exposure. Rev. Al Cockrell, who pastored in Kansas City, called to tell me he had a player for me. The guy was 6'8" tall and had played basketball in the military. James Ransburg was part of my first recruiting class. He was joined by Steve Dillon (6'7" All-American from West Virginia), Jeff Burdge (6'7" player from Indiana), and Mark Trammell (another 6'8" player.) Suddenly, this team was tall, talented, and destined to national prominence.

While we quickly built our program, I was getting hundreds of invitations to speak at evangelistic rallies for Word of Life, churches, athletic banquets, and chapel services in Christian schools. The Word of Life rallies averaged 50 to 100 churches participating. Suddenly, God was placing me on the national scene. This was exactly what I envisioned for my life calling.

• • • •

In 1976, my dad came to see my team play. Keep in mind, he hardly ever saw me play in high school. He was usually too drunk to go to my games; but after he got saved, God changed him. He made many trips to Chattanooga to see me as a player in college. And when I began coaching in college, I knew he was my biggest fan.

One night after a game we won, he came into my office and closed the door.

"Son, I want you to know that I am proud of you," he told me. To have this affirmation and expression of love from my dad was a moment that I will treasure forever.

On Thanksgiving weekend, we always hosted an eight-team holiday tournament. I looked forward to this special time when Mom and Dad would come to Chattanooga, see the games, and enjoy Thanksgiving with us.

However, in 1977, Dad and Mom planned to arrive on Wednesday night. Dr. Jack Hudson, one of Dad's favorite preachers from Charlotte, was scheduled to speak at the morning Thanksgiving service before games began. They planned to arrive around midnight and stay at a Day's Inn, about one mile from our house.

At 7:00 a.m., I received a call from Mom, who could hardly speak.

"Ronnie, please get over to the hotel," she cried. "Something is wrong with Dad."

I scrambled quickly to get dressed. I rushed out of the house and arrived at the hotel within five minutes. When I saw the door open on the second floor and members of the Sheriff's department walking out, I knew this was not good.

I rushed in the room. Mom grabbed me!

"Ronnie, he's gone! Dad is dead," she cried.

We stood there embracing one another as I looked over her shoulder and saw my dad, lying on his back, eyes half open, and jaw twisted.

"Mama, listen! 'To be absent from the body is to be present with the Lord,'" I whispered. "Dad's in Heaven!"

Pat held Mom while I walked close to the bed. My heart broke. I began to cry uncontrollably. My dad was gone.

It seemed like just yesterday we were with each other. In fact, I called my dad in the middle of October and told him that I had two tickets to the Clemson–Maryland football game. One of my best friends, Morgan Hout, was on the coaching staff at Maryland. Dad met me at Death Valley (the nickname of Clemson's stadium) and we saw a great Maryland team beat the Tigers. After the game, Dad and I went into Maryland's dressing room to meet Morgan.

As we left the stadium that day, I remember walking up a steep hill. Dad had to stop. We paused under a tree while Dad got his breath and let the chest pains subside. He lived with this condition and had so many episodes that we got used to it. Dad didn't go to doctors, so a heart procedure was out of the question for him.

"Ronnie, he must have died in his sleep," Mom said. "I got up to go to the bathroom about 5 a.m. It was dark and I didn't want to wake him. But about 6:45, I touched him and his skin was cold."

It was over! At the young age of 55, my dad was in eternity with the Lord.

The funeral home came to get his body. They prepared it and flew it on the airplane to Charlotte. Meanwhile, I took Pat and Mom to the airport. I stayed back to get some friends to watch our two little girls. Then I started the 6 hour drive to Blacksburg in my dad's car.

Three days later, I preached my dad's funeral sermon in the First Baptist Church of Blacksburg. This was difficult. For the first time in a long time, I realized that there were still things in my life that I could not fix or conquer.

Even though things were going so well for me and I was beginning to feel like a champion, I would have traded it all for another day with Dad.

I returned to Chattanooga after the tournament. When I went to practice, the players presented to me the championship trophy they had won in the Thanksgiving Tournament. They dedicated the wins to me and gave me the trophy, which I have kept since that day. This was the beginning of many championships the TTU teams gave Lefty and me.

CHAPTER 10

BUILDING THE FOUNDATION

Truthfully, we began laying the foundation in our second year. The first year was spent playing with the guys who were inherited. Even though the team, led by Danny and Victor, won 17 games, the year was a transition year. It was my first year as a head coach. It was the first year our staff worked together. It was also a year when many outstanding freshmen began their careers.

During the initial season, I went out on the recruiting trail to find a couple of front–court players to play with our outstanding guards: Dan Smith, Jerry Adams, and Mitch Steiner. I loved my players. Jerry Adams was special to me almost like a son. I still remember Adams' girlfriend, Tamara, hanging around the gym. She was a beautiful, dark complexioned girl. Girls easily distract players, but I would have issues with a guy if he didn't pursue a girl. Jerry was in love with Tamara, but many times a date with Jerry consisted of going to the gym and rebounding while he shot free throws and perimeter jumpers—my kind of guy! This kind of player helps build a foundation and tradition of championship basketball.

I recruited two players, James Ransburg (6'8") and Steve Dillon (6'7"). James was a great scorer and became the greatest rebounder in school history. Dillon was one of the top 100 players in America during his high school senior season. Both became All-Americans at Temple. These two players, along with outstanding point guard Benny Polk and shooting guard David Montgomery, constituted my first recruiting class—and it was a good one!

With the leadership of Dan Smith and Victor Hazard, this Temple team went 28–6 in our second year, 1976–77. Ransburg and Dillon combined for 19.6 rebounds a game. We controlled the boards with these two freshman recruits.

Coach Glascock, a defensive genius, instilled an intense style of defense that limited our opponents to only 66.8 points per game. Applying defensive principles such as ball-side ball denial, open position on weak-side, ball-you-man triangle, and playing through picks resulted in an aggressive defense played with intensity. This defense became the basis for our success.

Our defensive style and intensity became trademarks that we proudly established.

Our defensive philosophy was defined, and the talent was there to take us to national prominence. We actually made it to the NCCAA National Tournament and lost in a semifinal game.

Though we seemed to regress in our third year (1977–78), we still went 25–9. Most coaches would be happy to have back-to-back 25-win seasons. We could blame a tougher schedule and a host of injuries, but the truth is we just didn't play well together.

The highlight of the year was our California trip to play in the Point Loma Classic in San Diego. We opened the tournament with a 75–65 win over California Baptist. In the semifinals we beat a strong Biola team by a score of 91–81. Approaching the championship game, we were tired and banged-up and lost to the host team (Point Loma Nazarene) by a five-point margin, 82–77. Before that loss, we had won 14 consecutive games. We finished the season 10-7.

During that stretch, we played an incredible game against NCAA Division II Armstrong State University on their court. We won that game 103–86. We were down 60–54 at the half, but early in the second half, Dan Smith scored 11 points in 2 seconds. Amazing! How did that happen? Well, Dan scored 2 points on a short jump shot and was fouled. The Armstrong coach protested the call, receiving a technical foul. Danny hit the first free-throw, but the coach kept the tirade going on the sideline. After two more technicals, the coach was ejected on his home court, before his home crowd, by his conference officials. (In 1978, a coach was not ejected until his third technical.) Danny hit four more free throws. On the inbounds play, Danny hit a quick jumper, which totaled 11 points in 2 seconds, a feat that may never be equaled.

The toughest part of 1977–78 was saying goodbye to our two seniors, Dan Smith and Victor Hazard. We lost the first game in the NCCAA tournament by one point. Even with 25 wins, we fell short of our goal of a national championship. These two players played a major role in establishing a legacy for our program. I will always be grateful to them and deeply regret that they could not get a championship ring. No two players who ever wore a Temple uniform deserved to get to our basketball promised land more than Dan and Victor.

I always knew that we had the best basketball program in Christian-college circles. Eventually, we believed that everyone in America would see Tennessee Temple as the leader in basketball among Christian colleges. I also knew that we had a distinct home court advantage in the national tournament.

In the 1970s, Tennessee Temple was the largest Christian college east of the Mississippi. We had more students on campus than Liberty and Cedarville. Basketball was strong. The National Christian College Athletic Association understood that. All of our home games were played in front of capacity crowds. The Dunkel Rating System had our program ranked first in the nation for several years; therefore, the NCCAA held their national basketball championship on our campus. The NCCAA made a great financial decision in this. Besides, no other Christian college in America had better media coverage at the time than Tennessee Temple.

Many coaches disgusted me as they complained about Tennessee Temple having such an advantage. The truth is very simple: We would have won national championships between 1979 and 1983 anyway, because we had the best teams in America among Christian colleges. I would have been proud to match our talent against any Christian college anywhere in the USA.

The championship finally came in 1978–79—the year that TTU climbed to the top of the mountain! Our team had incredible balance. Our point guard, Mitch Steiner, was a steady player who set a school record with 22 assists in one game. Jerry Adams, from Kingsport, Tennessee, was the other guard who finished his career with 1,511 points. Jerry was a greater shooter who averaged over 85 percent from the free-throw line. Ransburg and 6'7" Ted Manolis played the No. 3 and No. 4 positions interchangeably. James had a great scoring year at 701 points. Dillon played the post. This team averaged a phenomenal 48.3 rebounds-per-game.

This was a fun group! We enjoyed being together. Every road trip was a blast. On the road, I roomed with Darryl Burt, my administrative assistant. This team was forever playing tricks on me during road trips, such as placing smoke bombs in my room. Lefty was the mastermind, although Steiner and Adams were silent culprits.

The year was interesting because we played Lee College four times. We split with them in the regular season, but they beat us by one point for the conference title. However, two weeks later, we beat them for the national championship. During the season, we beat NAIA power David–Lipscomb College twice. The University of Tennessee at Chattanooga invited us to play in their annual Christmas tournament. In this Choo-Choo Classic, we were the only non-NCAA team. We lost to West Georgia by 7 points in the first game and then lost 93–92 to Delta State in the consolation game. We trailed by 19 points at halftime. Playing at UTC gave our program great exposure to the Chattanooga population.

A key player for us was Ted Manolis. At 6'7", Ted gave us three starters at 6'7" or taller. This talented front line combined with a group of great guards, led by Steiner and Adams. Recruiting Manolis was noteworthy. Driving to Atlanta one day, I stopped for gasoline. The attendant was playing basketball on a side goal. After talking with the 6'7" Manolis, I found out that he was unsaved and that he had at least two years of eligibility. I also recognized that he was a good shooter and got the impression that he was an exceptional leader.

The only hindrance was that Ted Manolis needed Christ! I invited Ted to visit me at TTU. He came for a visit, and I took him to church with me. That night, at the conclusion of the service, Dr. Lee Roberson did something very unusual. During the invitation, he asked for everyone who was saved to stand and for those who were not to remain seated. Even though we were supposed to have our eyes closed, I looked down to Ted, who was sitting on the pew. After the service, I talked with Ted in my office. Ted had a lot of baggage and simply did not have a personal relationship with Christ. That day in my office, Ted prayed and received Jesus.

It was exciting to see him enroll at TTU. Our staff and players witnessed a great change in his life. His family was very appreciative for what God was doing in his heart.

I recruited Ransburg by sending out five-thousand letters to pastors all across America. I asked pastors to respond if they had guys in church who could play basketball. Well, I got a lot of responses but none that I thought could help our program. Then I received a call from Al Cockrell, who was pastoring in Kansas City at the time. Al said he had a 6"8" African-American in his church who came on the bus route. He was married and had a son. He played 4 years while in the U.S. Army, but he wanted to go to college. When I found out that he made the all-military team overseas, I knew he could play.

In 1976, a stamp cost 12 cents and gasoline was 35 cents a gallon. With a tank of gas and a postage stamp, I got two frontline players who would take us to the promised land.

Our season started with a bang. We won our first nine games but lost 6 times in the next 16 games. During that stretch, we lost to Dyke College in the championship game at Cedarville's Yellow Jacket Classic. When we lost to Lee in our conference championship, we felt we were doomed to another 20-win season with no championship.

However, we got an at-large bid to the NCCAA national tournament. In the opening game, we played one of our season's best games to defeat Eastern Nazarene 96–67. In the semifinal game we faced Bethany Nazarene. This was a great game that we survived by winning 65–64.

Across the other bracket, our old rival, Lee College, won their semifinal game. We now had to face a team that had beaten us 2 out of 3 games, with the latest loss coming just a few days earlier. At a press conference, I stated that we could easily forget losing the conference title to Lee, if they would let us win the national championship.

The game was sold out. In fact, the gym was packed 2 hours before the game. Of course, this was nothing new to Temple. We always had capacity crowds in McGilvray Gym. We were fortunate to have the championship game on our home floor.

In the first half, Temple's largest lead was 8 points with 8:07 to play, 19–11. Lee pressed to get back into the game but missed its free throws, making only 6 of 12. James Ransburg and Ted Manolis each had 8 points at the intermission, and they controlled the backboards with 8 caroms apiece.

Steve Dillon stole the show in the second half. The 6'7" sophomore from Barboursville, W.Va. scored 16 of his game-high 20 points in the second half, including 5 as Lee mounted a furious rally.

Temple went up by twelve, 53–41, but the Lee press caused two straight turnovers. Lee converted both into points, cutting the lead to 8 and sending Jeff Burdge to the bench with 5 fouls. Burdge, another 6'7" forward, scored 10 points.

Dillon, who had 3 fouls himself, drove the baseline and scored with 6:34 remaining. He was fouled on the play and sank the free throw to put us back up by 9. He converted another drive moments later to put the Crusaders up by 11.

The closest the Vikings got in the final 6 minutes was 7 points. With just over a minute remaining, Ransburg hit both ends of a one-and-one. With only 53 seconds remaining, the Temple fans sensed victory and began to chant, "We're No.1!" We won, 75–64.

Ransburg and Jerry Adams, who both scored 12 points, were named to the national all-tournament team. Ransburg, who grabbed 44 rebounds in the 3 victories, was named MVP.

"I can't tell you how happy I am at this moment. This is the greatest thing that has ever happened to me in sports, and I'm so glad it happened because I love these kids," I told the press after the game. "I'm especially happy for the seniors. They're the greatest group of guys I've ever been around."

The moment we won the national tournament was unbelievable. Even today, it is hard to describe the feeling. Fans swarmed the floor. The celebration carried over into the streets on campus for hours after the game.

Allan Morris, veteran sports editor of the *Chattanooga News-Free Press*, stated, "I've seen happy and demonstrative crowds at sports events during 40-plus years of sports writing, but none beat the one at McGilvray Gym on Saturday night."

Even the usually reserved Dr. J. R. Faulkner, school vice-president, helped in cutting down the nets. Dr. Lee Roberson, pastor of Highland Park Baptist Church and president of Tennessee Temple University, visited our dressing room to pray with the team and rejoice in the championship.

I was named National Coach of the Year, but all the honors were shared, because together we had climbed to the top of the mountain and realized our goal. In four short years, we had built the foundation of a basketball program that set a standard for Christian colleges across America.

My coaching staff, led by Lefty and including Dave Melton, Brent Butts, and Daryl Burt, deserve most of the credit. However, building a championship program involved recruiting talented players who loved the Lord and committed themselves to the task. Finally, we never could have accomplished the goal without the resources and support of our school administration.

Dr. Roberson, nationally known Christian leader throughout the USA, came to all of our home games. When he came into the gymnasium, the student body always gave him a standing ovation. Dr. Roberson loved basketball, which was a great outlet for the four-thousand students at Temple. Dr. Roberson and I became close friends. We talked and prayed together. He let me know that he was fully supportive of our program.

No championship comes easily. Championships require a lot of vision, passion, commitment, and work; but when you win, everyone can celebrate. And we did a lot of that on March 17, 1979. Even my newspaper boy got in on the act by throwing 23 copies of the morning newspaper all over my yard the next morning!

As I look back, it is easy to answer the question people ask concerning multiple championships: Which one was the greatest? Without hesitation, I would have to say the first national championship was the most special. We worked so hard to get there. Tony Phelps, Jim Shoemate, Jerry Adams, Mitch Steiner, and Paul Zahn formed a special senior class. These guys became like my sons. Their commitment to Christ and basketball set a standard for our program.

CHAPTER 11

MAINTAINING A CHAMPIONSHIP PROGRAM

The next 6 years were tough! When we built the foundation and won our first championship in 1979, I didn't realize how high the expectation would be for us to maintain that level of success. In the next 6 years, we won the national championship three more times. We made the national tournament Final Four all 6 years. For 5 consecutive years we played in the championship game. We were expected to win! Finishing second was unacceptable.

During this time, I learned several things. First of all, I learned that maintaining success was more difficult than achieving it. Secondly, I learned how shallow championships were in the "big game of life." Thirdly, I learned how empty you become after it is all over. I remember how frustrated I became realizing that the satisfaction was very short lived. Nevertheless, we always went back to work to achieve success again.

In 1979–80, we lost more games than any year in my career, 13 losses. Many coaches would be elated with a 23–13 record. After having a big lead at the half, we lost in the NCCAA semifinals to Point Loma on a tip-in at the buzzer. To make the season even worse, we watched Liberty University win the national championship and cut down the nets. We played Liberty twice during the regular season and beat them: at home, 77–63, and at Liberty, 97–86. Dr. Jerry Falwell, chancellor of Liberty, sat behind our bench in Lynchburg, Va.

The year 1980 also marked the end of the James Ransburg era. Ransburg finished with the career scoring and rebound marks. The 6'8" Kansas City native led the school to a 105–36 record during his four years. Jeff Burdge, a solid 6'7" performer, and steady guards, Benny Polk and David Montgomery, also ended their careers. Benny was a tough, wiry point guard known best for his pesky defense and ability to lead the team. Many of his assists were to his high school teammate, Montgomery. David was a 6'2" shooting guard whose career was slowed by a knee injury. Jeff, Benny, and David were solid students and superlative athletes, with good spiritual testimonies. For those reasons, they were popular on campus with Crusader fans.

Among the conquered were traditional rival David–Lipscomb, a strong Central Wesleyan team, Southern Tech, a perennial NAIA power, Columbus College, unbeaten at the time of our match-up, and Tennessee Tech, a Division I team from the Ohio Valley Conference.

The biggest wins came on the road, including the bizarre victory over Tennessee Tech. The Crusaders embarrassed the OVC school, 95–77, in the opening game of UT-Chattanooga's Choo-Choo Classic. With 42 seconds to go, Coach Cliff Malpass pulled his team off the floor as a protest against the Southern Conference officials. The next day, Tennessee Tech fired Coach Malpass.

The win set up a clash for the championship against the UTC Mocs. This marked the first intercity basketball contest between the two schools. Temple led for most of the first half. The Mocs eventually won, 77–70, but Temple was never out of the contest until the closing seconds. Ransburg tallied 28 points against the Mocs. He and Dillon made the all-tournament team. However, a real shooting star in the tourney was freshman Jeff Smith. Against UTC, Jeff had 12 points on several long jumpshots.

The victory over Columbus came on the road, while Temple was struggling with a 7–5 worksheet. Columbus had opened with 5 straight wins and was leading the NCAA Division II in field-goal percentage. Temple won in overtime when sharpshooter Eddie Mullet dropped 2 free-throws with seconds to play.

This Crusaders team lost seven games on the home court. The year before, we had an unblemished home mark. When Lincoln Memorial defeated Temple in the Thanksgiving Tournament, it marked the first home defeat since February, 1977 and ended a school-record 22 straight home victories.

One year after a national championship, the Crusaders took a step backward; however, the decline didn't last long. I had an extremely successful recruiting year for the 1980–81 team. Transfers J. R. Lucas (Chipola Junior College) and Anthony Eubanks (Ole Miss) joined Tommy McMasters as the leading newcomers. With sharp-shooting junior Mullet and sophomore point guard Paul Pridemore, Temple had a guard duo with experience to form a strong nucleus.

I knew with Pridemore, Mullet, and these three recruits, we were going to be good. Remember, we still had All-American Steve Dillon

(6'8") and a steady 6'8" junior, Mark Trammell. Mark actually started at the post with Dillon until Eubanks, (6'7"), who was sitting out a semester to fulfill transfer rules, became eligible.

Eubanks was a starter as a freshman at Ole Miss, but he decided to transfer to study for the ministry. Evangelist Lester Roloff helped me recruit Anthony to Temple. He was one of the most sought-after players in the South. An all-state star at Nashville Hillsboro High, Anthony was the Nashville Player of the Year. I felt that with Anthony at power forward and Dillon at the post, Temple would have a devastating front line.

The 1980–81 season began with a bang. With only two returning starters, we went into December 7–1 and without Eubanks; however, in December the team hit a brick wall. In disastrous December, we lost 6 games. We were 7–7 and in a deep hole! Things got worse when our leading scorer and rebounder, Dillon, made terrible decisions and was dismissed from school. On the eve of the revelation of Dillon's departure, Temple was embarrassed by UTC, 101–78. To make matters worse, the game was locally televised.

Eubanks became eligible in January, and our team experienced spiritual and basketball revival. In January and February, Temple went 15–4. During that stretch Paul Pridemore became a seasoned leader. Mullet averaged 13.2 points-per-game while connecting on 52.5 percent of his field-goal attempts. J. R. Lucas, the 6'5" small forward from Citronelle, Ala., led the team in scoring with 14.7 ppg. He was also the team's leading rebounder with 7.5 rebounds-per-game. Freshman Tommy McMasters, whose play at times bordered on brilliance, averaged 9 points and 5.3 rebounds-per-game. At 6'3", Tommy was our best defender. He was capable of pulling down a rebound, taking it the length of the court, and dishing or popping a jumper. His versatility made him a triple threat. When Tommy McMasters came into the game, he was like a sixth starter. I knew we had all the components for another championship team. My coaching staff dedicated itself to not messing it up. After so many valleys in the previous year, we all needed a breath of fresh air.

Eubanks proved to be the Moses who led the team back to the NCCAA nationals with his powerful, in-your-face jams and shot blocks. Temple defeated Azusa Pacific (92–79) and Bethel College (69–59) to win our second national tournament in 3 years. Lucas was named MVP of the tournament after scoring 43 in the 2 games.

"At the first of the year, I thought we could win the whole thing, then I didn't, and then we did!" I was later quoted in a newspaper article.

Next came the 1981–82 season. This team returned all five starters plus four of our top five reserves. The campus was buzzing for good reason. The expectations were high, but I learned that we couldn't just roll the ball out on the court and win. Having dealt with success and learned from past failures, this team would become my all-time favorite. We had a solid group of guys with the experience and passion to win, with practically no baggage. Back were All-American seniors Eddie Mullet, J. R. Lucas, and steady Mark Trammell, a 6'8" senior. Our general, Paul Pridemore, who was like a coach on the floor, and Eubanks were still just juniors. Tommy McMasters was a proven sophomore. Again, the Lord blessed our recruiting efforts with Kevin Hicks, a 6'10" transfer from UTC. This team, blessed with height, had six players over 6'5" and a starting front line of 6'10", 6'7", and 6'5".

There's NOT a lot to say about this team, except they won. No other TTU team bonded better or were as entertaining to watch as the 1980–81 team. These Crusaders went 31–8. Even after a 1–3 start, no one doubted how good this team was. We had impressive wins over

NAIA powers Montevallo, Alabama, Huntsville, Carson–Newman, Lincoln Memorial, and NCAA Division II Columbus College.

The highlight of the season was a late-season road trip to Texas, where we defeated a strong Dallas Baptist team, 93–84. Few teams beat DBC on their home court. We easily outnumbered the DBC fans with members of church groups, Temple alumni, and special crowds from Dr. Gary Coleman's and Dr. Clyde Box's churches. They were amazed that we "brought so many fans on the road."

Going into the national tournament, we were the top-seeded team at 29–8. This TTU team proved the experts right by breezing through the national tournament. We defeated Spring Arbor by an amazing 64–40 score in the championship game, which was nationally televised on Pat Robertson's network. J. R. Lucas was the MVP for the second year in a row. I was named national Coach of the Year again.

The reason for this team's success was the talent-level at every position. Paul Pridemore was an exceptional point guard. Our shooting guard, Eddie Mullet was one of the finest perimeter shooters in America. Our front line, with NCAA Division I transfers Kevin Hicks (6'10") and Anthony Eubanks (6'6"), controlled the boards on both ends of the court. At 6'5", J. R. Lucas was the total package as a scorer, rebounder, and defender. Our inside-outside game, ability to hit perimeter shots, and inside power caused serious match-up problems. Among Christian colleges, this team had the best starting five in America, in addition to a strong bench. The team shot a school record 53.4 percent from the field.

The program was definitely headed in the right direction. Maintaining a national championship program 3 out of 4 years was a great stretch; however, we weren't finished yet!

In 1982–83, TTU won its fourth national championship. Winning 28 games against 7 losses should be an awesome year, but we had our problems. Though we had a 21-game winning streak at home and won 10 consecutive tournaments, we had our challenges. During the year, I became the winningest basketball coach in TTU history. We continued to get national notice with road wins at NCAA Division II Biscayne, Alabama–Huntsville, Ohio Northern, Lipscomb, and Carson–Newman.

Forward Brad Peters (6'5") and wing player Tommy McMasters were the heart of the team. We had recruited our most talented and best group of freshmen ever! These freshmen included Richard Pace (6'6") and Bobby Ross (6'6") from Newnan, Ga., Jeff Carter (6'6"), Brian Matthews (6'7"), and point guard Allen Carden. Along with cat-quick Reggie Clark, a junior–college transfer, they were very good additions to our team.

As a coach, I always felt a championship program was built around an athletic, intelligent, confident point guard. Most of my point guards became coaches. Allen Carden was probably the best all-around athlete I ever recruited. Allen and I still laugh about how I recruited him. On my first visit to his home, I brought graphs and charts to blow away any idea he may entertain about going to a junior college. In addition to signing with the Atlanta Braves to play baseball, he became a three-year starter at Temple.

Pace and Ross were teammates at Newnan. Bobby was a great shooter, while Richard, who played with his back to the basket, was an exceptional leaper. I was almost broke when they signed, because it took five trips to a Newnan steakhouse before they committed. They surely gained 20 pounds during that recruiting period.

However, seniors Eubanks, Hicks, and Pridemore were the nucleus of the '82–83 team. Paul was moved to shooting guard with the addition of Reggie Clark. Experience, defense, quickness, and rebounding characterized this team. The fact that we had eight freshmen on our roster gave us opportunity to coach.

One of the most memorable games in school history was played in Ohio at the Malone College tournament. Malone, who did not intend to play Temple or Ohio Northern in the opener, opted to play Baptist Bible of Missouri. In the first game we were pitted against one of the best defensive teams in America. We were playing Ohio Northern, coached by the legendary Gale Daughtery. Gale had been an assistant to Bobby Knight at Army. He was a defensive genius. Bruce Foster brought him to Temple on several occasions to implement his defensive philosophy in our program. Lefty learned most of his defensive mindset from Gale.

To many in the stands, the 21–19 halftime score seemed boring; however, when two excellent defensive teams play it is difficult to get an unchallenged look at the basket. It was the best defensive game I ever witnessed. We won the struggle by a 46–35 score. Baptist Bible upset host Malone. We won the tournament and Malone faced Ohio Northern after all, losing two games in its own tournament.

Tommy McMasters had a career night against Lee College, whom we beat 80–64. Tommy scored 21 points and had a phenomenal 10 steals on the defensive end. The teams met in the "Small Four" tournament with Bryan and Tennessee Wesleyan. Led by Eubanks' 21 points and Hicks' 16 points, Temple beat Bryan in the championship game.

Temple also beat Alabama-Huntsville twice, winning the first contest 69–60 to halt a seven-game UAH winning streak. A road win against Biscayne in Miami (67–53) was another stunner. Biscayne had only 5 losses, all coming against NCAA Division I teams. Temple actually beat them worse than Texas and almost as bad as Houston. McMasters had 16 points in that game, while Pridemore chipped in 15.

The Crusaders had a torrid stretch, winning 16 of 18 games, which ranked them as the No.1 Christian college team in America, going into a game with Berry College. During that time, Tommy McMasters broke a school record with 13 steals against a strong Lincoln Memorial team. We were 25–7 going into the national tournament before THE BOTTOM FELL OUT!

Just before the national tournament began in 1983, three of our players went to a party and were caught drinking alcohol. Of course, this was scripturally wrong and a violation of our Christian-College handbook. Being raised in an alcoholic home, I was especially distressed. The incident occurred the weekend before the national tournament. We were faced with a disciplinary decision. As a coach, it would be easy to slap the guys on the wrist and ignore the situation. After all, two of the players involved were starters, and the other was our top reserve. To make matters worse, our starting point guard, Allen Carden, had left to join the Atlanta Braves in spring training. Our reserve guard, Craig Parr, had been sick all week.

The school easily could have dismissed the students and kicked them out of school. However, I appealed to the administration to allow them to stay, if I could administer the punishment. With the favor of our school president, Dr. Lee Roberson, I recommended that the three players be suspended from playing in the national tournament but be allowed to remain in school. Also, we made them sit on the bench with white shirts and ties. I wanted to show compassion while teaching them, and our entire student body, that obedience to the principles of God's Word was far more important than a game.

I knew that this decision could be detrimental to our team's chances of winning a national tournament. I also knew that our team would suffer the most from this decision. Sin affects many people. Sometimes the consequences of sin fall upon a team, a family, a student body, a church, and a nation. What began as a group of young people wanting to engage in a little pleasure was about to impact a student body of four-thousand people. These kids made selfish decisions that affected a lot of people. Every Christian needs to value and make good decisions. We had sold our team on the concept that when one succeeds, we all succeed. Since basketball is a team game, there are no heroes for making last-second shots. Likewise, we taught them that if one fails then we all fail. This principle was about to come alive as a lifelong lesson to the '82–83 team.

The Bible also teaches that God will honor them who honor Him. This team, these coaches, and an entire student body were about to see a miracle! We were positioned to see what determination, desire, and the awesome hand of God could do when our strength is gone!

In the first game, we were playing Bryan College. They had beaten us once during the regular season. Lefty and I knew that if we could win the first game, then we had a chance.

At the half, we had a slim one-point lead, 28–27. One of our starters, Craig Parr, was our fourth guard and had not played a full game in 2 years. He contributed 10 points in the game. Regulars Paul Pridemore (14 points), Anthony Eubanks (6 points), and Kevin Hicks (22 points) contributed two-thirds of our offense. Reserve forward Brad Peters scored 10 points. But it was Hicks who was a dominant factor inside, hitting on 9 of 11 from the field and grabbing 9 rebounds. Eubanks scored only 6 points, but he had 2 powerful

Ronnie, 1st grade.

Senior High school picture. Ronnie was president of the student body of Blacksburg High School, 1962-63.

Blacksburg High School Graduation, Blacksburg, SC - 1963.

Blacksburg High School football. Ronnie was captain and MVP his senior year.

Ronnie was quarterback his senior year of high school. Season record was 7–2.

Graduation from TTU, 1967, Ron recieved a Bachelor of Arts degree.

TTU Team media guide. Anthony Eubanks (left), Paul Pridemore (right), star players and captains of 1982 national championship team.

1981-82 Basketball

NCCAA 1980-81 CHAMPS

Goodnews Broadcaster 1979. Coach Ron Bishop surrounded by several members of first NCCAA national championship team.

Ron's coaching years at TTU, won four national championships.

United States Senate
WASHINGTON, DC 20510

April 10, 1985

Coach Ron Bishop
Coach DeWayne "Lefty" Glascock
c/o Randy Stem
Box 2041
Tennessee Temple University
Chattanooga, Tennessee 37404

Dear Ron and DeWayne:

It is my pleasure to join with your family and friends
to commend you for ten years of outstanding service to
Tennessee Temple University. Your dedication and talent have
been a credit to your school, and your leadership and
example have been a positive influence on the lives of the
young players you have coached.

I wish I could join you on this occasion, and I feel
sure that this event will be a tremendous success. My
best wishes to you and your families.

Sincerely,

Albert Gore, Jr.
U.S. Senator

AG/lab

City of Chattanooga

April 11, 1985

Coach Ron Bishop
Tennessee Temple University
1815 Union Avenue
Chattanooga, Tennessee 37404

Dear Coach Bishop:

It's a privilege to congratulate you on your excellent record over the past ten years. Temple has achieved a great name in the field of athletics, and I know this would not have been possible were it not for your outstanding leadership. I'm happy this year's team has chosen to honor you and Coach Glascock at the April 23 banquet. I regret that my schedule does not permit me to be with you for the occasion. However, I'm happy to be use this method of adding my commendations to the many others I know you will receiving. Chattanooga is proud of the Crusaders and proud of you!

With best wishes, I am

Very truly yours,

Gene Roberts

GR/jn

Congratulations, Ron.

Ron and Pat with daughters
Robyn and Rhonda.

Andres Paz (left), director of Word
of Life Argentina. Joe Jordan (right),
best friend and former teammate,
Executive Director of Word of Life
Institute.

Anthony Douglas (left), plays professional ball overseas. P.J. Brown
(right), 12 yrs. NBA, currently
with the Chicago Bulls. Both traveled with Ron on an All Star trip to
Mexico.

Ron speaking to children at an orphanage in San Jose, Costa Rica.

Ron at orphanage interacting with children while handing out candy.

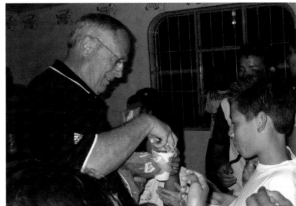

Andy Beal (pitcher), Andy Phillips (first baseman), Ron, Nardi Contreras (pitching coordinator). Baseball clinic in the Dominican Republic, sponsored by SCORE.

Ron and Pat with daughters Robyn and Rhonda and their families on first family mission trip together, Dominican Republic, June 2006.

Ron and Pat at Decatur Baptist Church, Alabama, being inducted into the Missionary Hall of Fame.

Ron's grandchildren, (left to right) Allyson, Chloe, Lex, and Ashley.

dunks and provided strong defense inside. Bryan's four inside players scored only 13 points against Eubanks, Hicks, and Peters.

We trailed the whole game by as many as 7 points; but when the dust had settled, we had beaten Bryan, 62–58. We had crossed a huge hurdle and were to face John–Brown University in the semifinal game.

Fatigue was the biggest concern we faced going into the John–Brown game. With a depleted squad, we had to play our starting 5 too many minutes. We played only 7 players, and the 2 reserves never scored. These players played with a lot of guts and heart, but they were tired.

Eubanks and Peters led a sizzling second-half spree that led us to an 81–66 win. Eubanks scored 22 points, while Brad had 16. Kevin Hicks, our 6'10" center, scored 20 point to collect 42 in the two games. As a team, we hit 51.6 percent of our field-goal attempts.

Just before game time, we got great news! Allen Carden, our starting point guard, received permission from the Atlanta Braves to leave spring training and join the team. Although Allen scored only 3 points, his presence gave us an emotional lift with his leadership and defense.

In the semifinal game, we played only 6 players. Next, we faced Grace College, led by 6'7" post player, John Boal, for the national championship. That we had expended so much energy just to get to the championship was a huge concern to our staff. Could we do it ONE more night? Could we dig deep and pull off an emotional victory?

Our 1983 championship game was a classic. Led by All-American Boal, Grace took advantage of our fatigue by pressing us on defense and pushing the ball. At the half, we were tied with them at 25. With four minutes to play, we trailed by 3 points, our biggest deficit of the game. Hicks scored 17 points and Pridemore had 11 assists to lead the Crusaders. Our All-American, Eubanks, finished with 14 points.

"I feel like this is the greatest of our four championships, especially with the adversity we faced," Coach Glascock stated. Besides the suspension of players, Tommy McMasters, one of our top players, was sidelined with a knee injury.

The championship in 1983 was our fourth national championship in 5 years. I agree with Lefty that it was the most gratifying. Our team and our student body learned that doing the right thing honors God. We saw a group of special guys play with emotion, heart, and passion. They came together and performed through adversity, disappointment, and fatigue. This team epitomized the concept of TEAMWORK. I will always remember Paul Pridemore, Kevin Hicks, Anthony Eubanks, Brad Peters, Craig Parr, and Allen Carden for their demonstration of how a true Christian athlete must perform under pressure.

The prospects for a good season looked good in the summer; however, things turned worse when Reggie Clark was suspended by the school, Craig Parr decided not to return, and Richard Pace decided to red-shirt because of a knee injury. Graduation had taken away Hicks, Eubanks, and Pridemore. Add these setbacks to the fact that our top recruit, JuCo All-American Bernard Baxter, a 6'7" North Carolina native, who averaged 24 points and 17 rebounds a game at Mitchell Junior College, was also suspended by the school early in the fall before our season began.

Suddenly, we thought we were faced with a major rebuilding job. We had little experience returning except seniors Brad Peters and Tommy McMasters and JuCo recruit Archie Barnes, a 6'5" junior. The rest of our team was sophomores and freshmen. Allen Carden, Bobby Ross, Jeff Carter, and Brian Matthews were all sophomores who would play a major role in the success of the '83–84 team. McMasters was coming off an injury, which limited him to 18 games. We were short on talent, experience, and height, but we felt good about the character of this team.

I always felt that we had the height, talent, and experience to win championships. However, this team was lacking, so we had to appeal to their desire and determination.

Archie Barnes was special to me. When I was recruiting him from Spartanburg Methodist Junior College, I told him we were also a Christian college. When I asked him about his conversion, he didn't seem to know what I was talking about. I explained that he could not come to TTU if he was not a Christian. On a campus visit, Archie received Christ—a true conversion that changed his life.

Archie was not a great offensive player at all. He loved playing on the defensive end of the court. I never had a player who loved to get into our opponent's offense like Archie. He was reckless and had an instinct for the ball. By teaming him with Tommy McMasters, Lefty and I knew we could win because of our defense.

Did we ever win! We got on a roll and won our first 15 games. In our opening game, Brian Matthews had 15 points and 15 rebounds. The 6'7" sophomore had help from another 6'7" sophomore, Jeff Carter, who scored 12 points, while claiming 8 rebounds. We connected 52.7 percent of our field-goal attempts and out-rebounded Bethel College 42–25.

We went on to top Spring Hill College, Belmont-Abbey, and Carson-Newman to win our Thanksgiving Tournament. Against Belmont-Abbey, sophomore point guard, Allen Carden, had 18 points

115

and played with outstanding intensity. After beating Carson-Newman 102-94, we knew the team was going to be special. Bobby Ross had 24 points against Carson-Newman, after scoring 20 against Spring Hill.

We continued to roll over Tennessee Wesleyan (61–47), Baptist College (87–67), Tusculum (120–97), Covenant (81–61), and Bryan (77-064). Against Tusculum, we had 6 players in double figures and set a school record by connecting on 70.9 percent of our field-goal attempts.

When we steamrolled over powerhouse University of Alabama-Huntsville, 66–46, we turned a lot of heads in the Southeast. This was our thirteenth consecutive win. We shot 55.1 percent from the field and held UAH to 10 points in the first 15 minutes of the second half. This team was establishing itself as the best defensive team in school history.

We reached the 14–0 mark with a 72–69 victory over Wooster College of Ohio. The defense created 20 Wooster turnovers, which actually won the game for the Crusaders.

Grace College, our opponent in the 1983 NCCAA final, was our next hurdle. With balanced scoring from McMasters (18 points), Matthews (17 points), and Barnes (13 points) we won, 76–66. Our stellar defense, led by Barnes' 6 steals and 12 rebounds, contributed significantly to the outcome of the game. This victory gave us a 15-0 record as we faced UT-Chattanooga as our next opponent.

The swarming defense of Temple frustrated the UTC scorers, led by future NBA standout Gerald Wilkins. With a swarming, intense defensive effort, the Crusaders forced the NCAA Division I team into 27 turnovers and trailed by only 7 points with 8 minutes remaining.

"Next to North Carolina and Alabama-Birmingham (both of

whom the Mocs had played), Temple's defense ranks above anybody we have played," Gerald Wilkins, who went on to a 13-year tenure in the NBA, said following the game.

After the UTC loss, we went on to win 16 consecutive games and entered the NCCAA national tournament with a 31–1 record. In the first game, we survived by beating Faulkner, 78–73. TTU struggled against the zone defense but finally pulled ahead, thanks to the outside shooting of Ross, McMasters, and Carden. Allen, with a "refuse to lose" mentality, scored all of his 13 points in the second half, while McMasters had 19 points. Ross chipped in 16 points.

In the semifinal game, we beat Western Baptist soundly, 74–56, led by McMasters' 20 points.

So, for the fifth time in 6 years, we were in the championship game, facing perennial NAIA power Biola from California. Biola was reputed to have a tenacious defense. Temple held Biola to 1 field goal in an 11-minute stretch in the first half. At the break, TTU held an 11-point lead.

However, Biola went to a match-up defense in the second half and limited Temple's looks at the basket. In the last 13 minutes of the game, we had very few good shots. Our only senior, Tommy McMasters, finished with 19 points—only 3 of which came in the final nine seconds of the game. We lost by 2 points.

"They took Tommy out of the game," remarked Coach Glascock. "Biola really focused on him late in the game."

I really thought we could win 4 straight national titles. Going into the final game 33–1 made the defeat even more devastating. To be that good and to come that close, losing by a single field-goal, will always haunt me. On the other hand, I never dreamed this team would win 33 games. It was still a season to remember!

I was nearing the age of 40, and God began to move in my heart about a life change. For several years, Lefty had begun to grow weary. I had to encourage him more than once to stay with me. We had no reason to leave Temple. We were at the top of the mountain and had built a program that was the envy of Christian colleges. Our basketball camps in the summer attracted 1,500 athletes each summer, which funded our program and gave us additional, personal income. Winning was no longer even satisfying. Our program was not going anywhere because we could go no higher at Temple. Besides, the university appeared to be undergoing some significant changes.

Prior to the 1984–85 season, I felt the rumblings at the school. In my opinion, some members of the Executive Committee were starting a movement to pressure Dr. Roberson out. I had been told that our scholarships would be cut. I believed that this was part of the power struggle to remove Dr. Roberson. I knew I did not want to be part of a program that was going to take steps backward. My premonition proved true, considering that the school had dropped 2,500 students in enrollment. These men, few of whom ever came to a game, were ignorant of the role intercollegiate athletics plays on a college campus, especially a campus that restricts students from other forms of entertainment. The gym filled to capacity on a night when students could rally together to scream, jump, wave arms, and make noise. This helped relieve the frustrations of our student body. The Executive Committee lacked the vision, academic credentials, public relation skills, and promotional ideas to move the school forward. This discussion drove prospective students to Cedarville and Liberty.

In my head, I knew I had to leave. Lefty was ready. I had alternatives, so the time was right. God gave me unrest about staying aboard a sinking ship, without the support of a lifejacket.

While coaching my final season, I began to process ideas of founding a sports–missions ministry. The missions trip that I went on in 1963 kept burning in my heart. God had changed my life and direction on that trip. Jim Gordon, founder and president of Sports and Cultural Exchange from Chula Vista, Calif., had invited me to go on one of his organization's sports ministries to Mexico. On that trip, I could see myself doing that for the rest of my life. I began to formulate ideas and wrote them down. At the Gospel Light Youth Camp in the summer of 1984, Steve Roberson and a group of friends came up with the name SCORE International. The acronym stood for "Serving Christ Our Redeemer Enterprises." As I prepared to coach my last season, I spent time planning for the founding of this new sports–missions ministry.

The 1984-85 season was a difficult decision, because Lefty and I knew it would be our last. We had a good group returning with Allen Carden, Brian Matthews, Jeff Carter, Bobby Ross, Richard Pace, Archie Barnes and two players who served their disciplinary time, Bernard Baxter and Reggie Clark. We added another JuCo All-American when we signed George Crittenden from North Greenville Junior College. This team was loaded with talent and appeared to be another national contender.

The team also included Greg Lockhart, Rick Burns, and Joey Roach. These guys were so special to me. Greg was 6'6" and from Signal Mountain, TN. His father, Joe, was a softball legend in Chattanooga. The family never missed a home game. They were a tight-knit family from the mountain. They were just good people, and Greg was a funny, quality guy to be around. Rick was a walk-on and another good guy, whom later became a close friend. After graduation, Rick worked for US Airways. Many times when I showed up at the

Chattanooga airport to take a flight, Rick always upgraded me to first-class. During the season, Rick encouraged guys to stay in line with his coaches' rules.

Joey Roach was not a talented player, but he thought he was. Joey's greatest contribution to our program was his intense desire to play and his willingness to sacrifice. If we had been a football team, Joey would have been an All-American linebacker. He never saw a situation that he was not willing to attack, despite the difficulty. His parents, Jo and Nolan Roach, were our team's biggest fans. Jo helped Teresa Glascock with the cheerleaders. She also kept the books at the business office, where I kept our camp money. She executed my requisitions for funds. Nolan pastored a small Signal Mountain church where Lefty attended. I preached there many times, carried the team there, and listened to Lefty sing. Joey and his family were my neighbors; they lived right behind our house on Richard Drive. We ate there a lot. I remember one holiday evening: Joey and Lefty bought some bottle rockets and they were firing them at my house. As I opened the sliding glass door to go on my deck, a bottle rocket flew over my head, through the sliding glass door, and into our dining room. Joey and his family became some of our closest friends.

The 1984–85 team was my last year. I do not recall many of the details, except that we had a very good season and made it back to the national championship game. Allen Carden was our leader. Allen tried to hold the team together. With Bernard Baxter, Reggie Clark, and George Crittenden, we were loaded with talent. However, keeping them focused on spiritual things was a challenge. Recruiting them together was my biggest mistake in coaching, but I never had a player whom I did not love and try to impact for Christ.

I have always had a heart for the lost. Ninety percent of my players showed a desire to live for God. Occasionally, I recruited lost people. I had a passion to share the Gospel with them, mentor them, and use basketball to impact their lives. I took a lot of heat from people who never saw my heart. My strategy sometimes did not work. In 10 years, we successfully mentored our players to serve God. James Ransburg, Jerry Adams, J. R. Lucas, Eddie Mullet, Archie Barnes, Allen Carden, Tommy McMasters, Benny Polk, and Paul Pridemore are just a few of the hundreds of players who wore the red and white. These guys distinguished themselves on the court. Most importantly for me, they learned to serve the Lord. Today, many of them are active leaders in church and serving the Lord with their families.

Yes, we made it back to the championship game. This was the eighth time we made the Final Four. Six times we played in the title game. Four times we won the national championship. This all happened in a ten-year coaching career. It was an amazing run.

We made it back to the tournament to regain the title we lost in 1984. However, again we came up short, losing to Point Loma by 2 points.

Now it was time to move on! I had built and maintained a successful basketball program at Tennessee–Temple University. God had another venture for me—another challenge—a career move that became a step higher in my service to the King.

ACCOMPLISHING GOD'S GAME PLAN

CHAPTER 12

NEW VENTURE

I knew God wanted me to leave Temple to start SCORE International. In December 1984, Lefty, John Zeller, Marty Benton, Pat, and I met with attorney Jim Perry to begin the legal process of making SCORE International a 501(c)3 non-profit religious foundation. Jim was a friend who graduated from Temple and actually played basketball for Coach Foster the season before my era began. He wrote our corporate papers, including the constitution and bylaws. In January 1985, SCORE International, Inc. was born!

The ministry was to be a sports–missions ministry to evangelize the lost, enhance the work of missionaries and national pastors, and edify and equip American teens on short-term missions trips. My prayer was that students would be impacted for missions the way I was.

Not long after I made the decision to found SCORE, the devil and the old flesh began to whisper in my ear. How would we make it? Would people support it? Would Pat and I survive this mid-life change, going from a steady income to "living by faith?"

In 1985, two things happened in March and in May, respectively, to cause me great discouragement and to further question my decision.

Just before the national tournament, Dr. J. R. Faulkner called my office. He called to inform me that the athletic director of Furman University was seeking permission to consult me about their vacant basketball coaching position. (I have often wondered why missionaries, pastors, and Christian school leaders do not follow this same ethical action that the world practices.) Furman University was a NCAA Division I school.

Furman, a Southern Baptist university in my home state of South Carolina, had just fired its coach for embarrassing the school with his profanity, recruiting, and behavior unbecoming of a professing Christian coach. Furman was looking for a successful, small, college coach who had Carolina roots and who could apply Christian principles to his life and work. They felt I met the criteria they sought in a coach. Being from South Carolina, a Furman scholar in high school, and from a Southern Baptist church, I felt I had a great chance to get the job.

Dick Sheridan, Furman athletic director, came to Chattanooga to interview me. The interview took place at a hotel restaurant in East Ridge on Sunday morning, just after the last national tournament. It went extremely well. Coach Sheridan told me the things that I needed to do to become a finalist.

This was a battle! As I walked out of the interview, I knew that my basketball career was over. I knew that God had positioned me to direct SCORE International. Instead of the financial security and dream of NCAA Division I coaching, I walked away! I drove to the airport

126

and flew off to Oklahoma to preach—and I NEVER looked back. Few people ever knew I had this opportunity!

A month later, I announced my resignation from Tennessee Temple. I immediately began to concentrate on recruiting my first team to go overseas with SCORE International. However, I still faced another challenge. The next president of Tennessee Temple University wanted to interview me about staying at TTU and continuing coaching. Dr. J. Don Jennings invited me to his office. He asked me to reconsider my resignation. He even offered me a $10,000 raise to stay. Of course this was a serious and significant raise. I had gone too far, though, and I knew SCORE would be my last place of ministry. I looked at Dr. Jennings and said that my mind was made and my heart was committed to SCORE.

"Ron, SCORE will <u>never</u> score!" he said. I was stunned. Never in my wildest dreams did I anticipate such a statement. I knew God was confirming my vision. I saw this as a real challenge. Knowing God's hand of leadership, I was determined to make SCORE score!

In May 1985, I resigned from the positions of athletic director and head basketball coach at Tennessee Temple University. God gave me 10 great years at TTU. We had taken a good program and made it a championship program.

A new venture had begun in my life. SCORE International started slowly. We recruited a basketball team to go to Mexico. Though it was the first trip, God gave us a group of about 15 players and support personnel to go to Mexico City. From the largest city in the world, we traveled to many cities, such as Colima, Leon, Pachuca, Guadalajara, Queretarro. We played before large crowds, preached the Gospel, and saw many saved. I didn't know it then, but this ministry would soon take off. It went from a $30,000 first-year budget with one overseas trip to a multimillion-dollar budget taking groups almost every week of the year to many countries.

As I look back over my life, it has been amazing that God could call me from a dysfunctional home in a small town to cities around the world. All along the way, God has blessed and success has followed me. I have preached in Mexico City, Buenos Aires, Rome, Paris, Moscow, Prague, Nassau, Lucerne, and many other great cities. I was able to preach to millions on television and to thousands in person.

People often ask me if I miss coaching. I easily answer with an emphatic and resounding NO! You see, when I retired from coaching, I began to take thousands of athletes on hundreds of teams around the world to preach and bring souls to Christ through sports. I have never had much time to think about missing college coaching.

I am always amazed to watch God's sovereign hand upon my life. In September 1985, a local television sports anchor, Randy Smith, called me. Randy told me that his color commentator partner for televising the University of Tennessee-Chattanooga basketball games had moved on to a larger market. He asked me if I would like to do three games on local television.

"You are a good speaker, you know the game, and I'd like for you to work with me," Randy stated.

Wow! I thought this would be an awesome opportunity for me. It would keep me near the game I love and grant me access to college coaches and college players for my ministry. This broad exposure would make my new ministry flourish—all in addition to how much I would enjoy this new assignment. I honestly believe that God's favor has been on every endeavor of my life.

Can you imagine what it's like to sit courtside, talk into headsets, watch a great game, analyze it, comment on what you see, and get paid to boot? After the first year of television, I did six games. The next year I worked ten games. Then I was doing twenty games a year. My work on television took me to Rupp Arena, Shoemaker Center, Alexander Coliseum, and Cameron Indoor Stadium. During a span of 10 years, I worked games for SportsSouth, Fox, ESPN regional, the Sunshine Network, and CBS affiliates. I did games for Georgia Tech, Kentucky, Cincinnati, Southern Mississippi, Memphis, Duke, South Florida, Texas Christian, North Carolina State, and all the Southern Conference teams. This venture was the most enjoyable, fulfilling, and exciting thing I have ever done. I met coaches, players, athletic directors, and sports information directors. God used these relationships to give me access to the people who accelerated the growth of SCORE International.

I began to be a speaker at NBA chapels and college basketball chapels. I found this ministry to be very exciting—sitting in an NBA room with players who were looking for the purpose and encouragement to stay focused on Christ. I have done chapel for the Heat, Cavaliers, Hawks, Magic, Timberwolves, Nets, and Kings. I never went into chapel with a camera. I never asked for a phone number or autograph. I knew God put me in that place with the Word of God to share a thought from Heaven. I did not approach these young, famous, multimillionaires with admiration. Rather, I saw them as young men with so many needs, weaknesses, temptations, and problems. They needed a touch from God. I was there as God's man to deliver God's Word—that was my calling.

Winning games was such an important part of my life. Now God had put me in places to impact so many lives. He taught me a new kind of winning, a new challenge, and a new focus.

• • • •

Another illustration of God's sovereignty occurred in 1986. I was planning a basketball trip to the Philippines. I had heard how much the Filipino people loved basketball; but just after the first of the year, the president of the Philippines, Ferdinand Marcos, was deposed. This created a lot of unrest. Fighting broke out, and as I watched the news, I became convinced we could not go there.

But where should we go? We had begun raising funds and recruiting players. We did not have much time. Then, for some inexplicable reason, Joe Jordan came to my mind. Joe and I were college basketball teammates. We played together, prayed together, and determined to serve God with our lives; however, I had not seen or spoken with him in over 20 years. After graduation, I knew Joe had gone with Word of Life to start a ministry in Argentina. That's it! I knew Joe still had a burning passion for the souls of men. If any missionary could understand the concept of sports evangelism, Joe could.

I got the telephone number of Joe Jordan in Argentina; and on my first attempt, I reached him. Joe was surprised to hear from me, and we talked quite a while before I shared my dilemma with him.

"Absolutely! Bring it on," Joe said. "We have a place for the team to stay. We have transportation and we can give you meals. My staff can get games in Buenos Aires."

When I hung up the phone, I knelt to thank God for His direction and answer to prayer. As we began to plan, I knew God was about to do something BIG!

In 1986, as we arrived at Word of Life in Monte, I was swept away by the enormity of the work Joe had established. Joe had a great deal of people close to him, most of whom he led to Christ and mentored. The Bible Institute had approximately five-hundred students from every

Spanish-speaking country. On our first day on campus, we went to chapel. I have never been with a student body so energized by the Bible. The music was awesome. I sensed an electricity in the air unlike any Christian college in America.

Students at the Bible Institute were there for 3 or 4-year programs. They studied hermeneutics, eschatology, ecclesiology, evangelism and missions, Greek, systematic theology, pneumatology, Christology, the Pauline epistles, the Gospels, Old Testament and New Testament survey, etc. Everyone was involved in weekend ministry. This was unlike any Bible institute in the world—at least unlike any started by Baptist missionaries

The campus had a chapel auditorium, an infirmary, a gymnasium, a library, classrooms, dormitories, married housing, a dining hall, elementary and secondary school, a lake, livestock, tennis courts, basketball courts, and soccer fields. It was amazing and truly a model institution preparing Hispanic students to reach the world.

At Word of Life I met students from around the world. They became fascinated and involved in our ministry. They mingled with the basketball team that we took to play games in 1986. They attended games and saw how sports evangelism attracted crowds of spectators, officials, newspapers, and television. Suddenly, I was swamped by students who told me that they wanted to bring SCORE teams to their own country, when they completed their studies.

Therefore, we immediately established relationships with Costa Rica, Brazil, Ecuador, Chile, Honduras, Panama, Guatemala, Paraguay, Uruguay, Bolivia, and many other countries in Central and South America. Now I had the contacts, personal relationships, and invitations to keep SCORE International busy throughout my lifetime.

We have seen the definite favor of God upon our ministry through this connection. Our ministry suddenly became global as we began to take teams to Argentina, Brazil, Costa Rica, Panama, Chile, Curacao, and Guatemala. I have always credited the 1986 Word of Life trip to Argentina for our global expansion.

The trip also renewed my close relationship with Joe Jordan. Joe and I became celebrities in the sports world in Argentina. We played the top professional clubs in Argentina, including the Argentine National team, and conducted basketball clinics for coaches. Some of our acquaintances are now the leaders of the basketball federation that led the Argentine team to the gold medal in the 2004 Olympics, embarrassing the USA team, consisting mostly of NBA players.

The teams that we took to Argentina had some of the top players in the USA, including several NBA players. The result was to preach the Gospel to thousands in arenas as well as on national television.

The hand of God was obviously on our sports–missions ministry from its inception. Later, Joe Jordan became executive director of Word of Life International, and I became a board member of WOL. Because of this relationship, SCORE International had the opportunity to partner with WOL missionaries in fifty foreign countries.

Little did I realize when we attached "International" onto SCORE, Inc. that we would have more than a Caribbean or Central American ministry. Rather, our teams have gone to Russia, Cuba, the Czech Republic, Trinidad, Italy, Brazil, Australia, Switzerland, Portugal, Chile, Costa Rica, and many others. SCORE truly became International after 1986.

• • • •

Wow! Rupp Arena is quite a basketball venue. Yes, I have been to Cameron Indoor Stadium. Actually, I saw North Carolina play Duke there. I must admit to watching the "crazies" of the Duke University student body doing zany things in unison with their funny hair and blue painted bodies.

Sitting courtside in Rupp Arena with 25,000 Kentucky fans is the pinnacle of basketball dreams. I worked as a color commentator and analyst for college basketball on television. Rick Pitino was the Kentucky head coach. His assistants included Tubby Smith, Billy Donovan, and Herb Sendek. All three became successful head coaches at NCAA Division I universities.

My dad was a huge Kentucky fan. He idolized Adolph Rupp. Coach Rupp was THE greatest coach of his era. Simply being at the arena named for this Hall of Fame coach was my honor. However, I wasn't just there—I had the credentials to gain access to every nook and cranny of the building.

The university gave me eight guest tickets; but I was so rushed getting to Lexington, I didn't have time to call any friends. I asked the guys in the production truck to go outside and sell them. You must understand that Rupp Arena is ALWAYS sold out. Tickets are either inherited or sold at a premium. The tickets that I inherited were on the top row, so I was shocked when the guys came back with $400. We ate well after that game.

The most memorable game I ever did was at the Citadel in Charleston, SC. Citadel is the military school of South Carolina. They were hosting Duke University, who later won the NCAA National Championship that year. Duke's starting lineup was Bobby Hurley, Grant Hill, Thomas Hill, Billy McCaffrey, and Christian Laettner. The great Mike Krzyzewski was the head coach. The most significant thing about that evening was not the game, which the Blue Devils won by 30 points, but the fact that it was THE night that President George Herbert

Walker Bush initiated the Desert–Storm war by bombing Baghdad.

Just before the tip-off, the public address announcer informed the fans that the bombing had begun. The cadets cheered wildly for several minutes. That evening, ABC's "Nightline" showed a clip of our television satellite feed with the reaction of the cadets. I wondered if anyone in the country was watching the game that night.

As I look back over my career, I can see the hand of God superintending the right connections to orchestrate His game plan for my life. The television gig placed me on a national scale, put me on a first-name basis with national coaches, and gave me access to some of America's greatest athletes. Truly, this was a God-thing.

Looking back to my roots, I think the Lord has blessed me in amazing ways. Consider that Rupp Arena had more fans than live in my county back in South Carolina. I've gone from little Blacksburg to Kentucky, Duke, Georgia Tech, Georgia, Tennessee, Alabama, and Mississippi State—Amazing!

I was on no quest for success; I had no personal agenda. I only wanted to become a winner. I vowed not to be a loser in life. If I succeeded in life, then I could accomplish a significant and meaningful work for God. I could have a platform to impact people. To me—winning was everything!

As an athlete, I was prepared to face a lot of adversity. Every athlete has entertained thoughts of quitting when things got difficult. I considered quitting so many times in high school and college. I am glad I never did!

Working through adversity prepared me for the multitudes of painful ministry moments. These are times to be tough! Everyone who serves God understands that ministry is NOT what it is always cracked up to be. There will be pain, hurt, discouragement, ridicule disloyalty, gossip, slander, division, dissention, and many other emotional attacks. Taking hits by linebackers, being cussed out by coaches, hearing insults from fans, and being humiliated by teammates prepared me to persevere and finish FAITHFUL.

CHAPTER 13

PASSION FOR THE SOULS OF MEN

One of the things my mentor, Coach Foster, taught me was a passion for the souls of men. I have often heard Joe Jordan say that only two things on earth are eternal—the Word of God and the souls of men. Bruce made every road trip an evangelism explosion.

His influence created in me a zeal to pursue pagans and share the Gospel. That influence carried over to my days as head coach at Tennessee Temple University. After all, my life verse was Romans 1:16, and I was NOT ashamed of the Gospel of Christ. I wanted every player I coached to catch that same passion for evangelism.

I remember on one occasion stopping to pick up a hitchhiker. Daryl Burt was driving our bus as we headed over to Central, South Carolina, to play Central Wesleyan College (now know as Southern Wesleyan). I spotted a hitchhiker on I-85 and told Daryl to pick him up.

I knew as soon as he climbed onto our bus that we were in for some fun. He was a real hippie, a throwback to the 1960s. He had long hair in a ponytail, a knapsack, dirty jeans, and a glazed look in his eyes, which indicated that he was living in fun land.

"What's your name?" I asked.

"Ritchie," he answered. "I'm from New York!"

"Well, we're not going that far," I blurted. "But we will take you north to Greenville. Grab a seat."

I watched as he sat right in the center of our team. When I looked back Minutes later, he was surrounded by guys 6'10", 6'8", 6'6", and a few shorter guards. We had black players, white guys, Southerners, and a few Yankees. All began to quiz him about his "eternal" destination.

"Oh, yeah, I know I'm going to Hell!" we heard him say. "Yep, I'm a sinner for sure."

I know this guy was wondering how he ever got on this bus! But later the conversation calmed long enough for a little laughter and joking. He seemed to enjoy the ride but occasionally had to endure more quizzing about where he was going to spend eternity.

As we neared the place where we were to turn off I-85 and head to Central, I told Ritchie that we were a college basketball team headed for a game. I explained that this was as far north as we were going and that we were turning off I-85 to eat our pre-game meal at a restaurant.

"Oh, I'd love to go with you," he exclaimed. "I haven't seen a college game in years. And I'm in no hurry to get to New York. Think I could tag along?" he asked.

"Sure, I guess," I muttered with some astonishment and a lot of amusement. "Well, maybe he will get saved. Maybe he is under conviction," I thought.

Later, when I discovered he had no money, I knew it wasn't conviction but a lot of hunger that drove him to hang with the team. Regardless, we were having fun with our adopted hippie!

Inside the restaurant, the patrons stared at the team as we filed inside, which wasn't unusual. Any group of tall basketball players, clean-cut, and dressed in red blazers and gray slacks will always got second looks. People knew we were a college team.

This time was different, however. I noticed people looking at Ritchie. It was so obvious. Twelve tall, clean-cut, college athletes, being followed by a dirty hippie with long hair in a ponytail and a knapsack on his back, brought plenty of stares; this caused me to smile.

While we were eating, a little lady came over to my table.

"Are you the coach of this team?" she asked.

"Yes, ma'am, I am," I answered.

"Well, I want to congratulate you. You have a good-looking group of boys," she said. "They are so well groomed and it really is impressive. You don't see boys like this anymore."

I almost laughed as she did a double take as she passed by Ritchie. She's probably still trying to figure out how he fit into the group.

I should have guessed that Ritchie didn't have money for the game, so I told him to grab our medicine kit and walk with us as we passed inside the gym. I know the security officer was amused. Here came the Tennessee Temple University ("Distinctively Christian") basketball team—clean-cut, shaven, well-groomed, and dressed for success— followed by a stinking, dirty, long-haired hippie, carrying our medicine kit.

This road game was over two-hundred miles from our campus. We had very few fans there besides our typical church following, led by a local church pastor who graduated from Temple. When the other team scored, the home crowd of over two-thousand cheered loudly. Whenever Temple scored, one dirty, long-haired hippie stood alone, clapping like a little kid.

The game was tight and came down to the last minute. We were down by one point. We had the last possession and the clock showed 8 seconds. After a timeout, we designed a play for James Ransburg. The 6'8" post player hit a turn-around bank shot at the buzzer, and we won!

Our entire team ran onto the court, grabbed our starters, danced around, and ran off the court together, celebrating wildly. We regrouped in our dressing room, sang "Victory in Jesus," prayed, and continued to celebrate, when suddenly, I noticed Ritchie. I told a couple of players to grab the hippie and throw him in the showers.

I realized that Ritchie had no other clothes, but he didn't seem to mind, considering this was his first shower since heaven knows when.

When I got onto the bus, the team was still celebrating. I noticed Ritchie as he sat there, soaking wet and laughing with the guys.

"Ritchie, this is I-85. We'll be heading south now," I said as we pulled over.

"Coach, thanks for a great evening," he said as we got off the bus together. "Ritchie, wouldn't you like to be saved?" I asked, standing beside the bus on I-85.

"Coach, I'm not ready," he said. "But, Coach, I want you to know that these guys are a lot of fun. I've laughed so much. Coach, I'm gonna think about it."

"Ritchie, don't wait too long. I'm praying for you!"

I have never forgotten Ritchie, the hippie. I hope and PRAY that I will see him in Heaven someday. If so, it will be because of the power of the Gospel and the Word of God. I also believe it will be because he saw some authentic Christianity that night. He saw no alcohol, no drugs, no filthy jokes, or profanity. What he saw was a group of guys who played a game and had a passion for his soul.

My mentor—Coach Bruce Foster—powerfully portrayed that passion before me.

• • • •

Preaching in a revival one Easter in Vinton, Virginia, I met a guy named Roscoe. Roscoe came in, sat in the back, and listened. He caught my eye, and I launched a gospel bomb in his direction. I just knew he would come forward and get saved.

He looked like a sinner. He carried an odor, had long hair, facial hair, and dirty clothes. He seemed to be a candidate for salvation.

I was surprised when he didn't come forward after the sermon. Standing at the door, I shook hands with people as they departed. Roscoe was one of the first, since he was on the back row.

"What's your name?" I asked.

"Roscoe," he answered.

"Roscoe, are you saved?" I just knew he was lost.

"Yep! Got saved this morning. I prayed with you when you prayed," he stated.

I was stunned!

"Really? Well, you need to come forward and share with the congregation. Are you coming back tonight?"

"Sure," he said.

"Well, will you come forward during the invitation to share what God did for you?"

"I'll do it!"

"Great!" I said.

That night I preached my message and gave the invitation. Down the aisle walked Roscoe.

"I'll take care of this," I said to the pastor.

"Roscoe, why are you coming forward?" I asked.

"Well, you told me to come," he deadpanned.

"Sure. OK. So, will you tell the audience what happened this morning?" I asked.

"I will," Roscoe replied. And he did. He told them he prayed and received Christ. Everyone was excited and thrilled at his testimony.

The next night I was greeting people as they arrived early. I noticed a "new" guy. I went over and introduced myself.

"Hey, I'm Roscoe!" he exclaimed.

"Roscoe? Wow, I didn't recognize you."

Roscoe had cut his hair, shaved, and wore clean clothes. He even wore some strong men's cologne. He was definitely a NEW man from the inside out.

When I concluded my sermon that night, Roscoe headed down the aisle.

Oh, no, I thought, he has lost it! I knew that wasn't possible, but I thought maybe he was confused.

Halfway down the aisle, he reached into his pocket and pulled out a pack of cigarettes. Arriving at the front, he handed the cigarettes to me and blurted out, "Here, preacher, you can have them."

"Roscoe, I don't want those."

"Well, I'm giving them to God!"

"Roscoe, He doesn't want them either," I said.

I was amazed at how God was working. I never preached against cigarettes, long hair, or beards; but God was changing him. Roscoe became living proof of II Corinthians 5:17, as God began changing Roscoe into a new creation in Christ Jesus.

The next night, I preached on soul-winning. I encouraged everyone to go out and compel their lost friends to come to the revival. Most of the Baptists who had been saved a very long time were challenged; however, I could tell Roscoe was intently focused on the challenge. After all, he was a babe who, like a sponge, was taking to heart every word of the message.

As we began the singing on the last night, Roscoe showed up in the vestibule. When the doors swung open, I watched Roscoe herding about twenty-five of his friends, pushing them through the doors to find seating in the rear of the auditorium. This amused the choir, as they watched this motley crew take their seats.

I preached and gave the invitation. Roscoe immediately sprang into action. He began to push his twenty-five pagan friends into the aisle and down to the altar. When I met them down front, it was exciting.

"Preacher, tell 'em what you told me Sunday," Roscoe exclaimed. "These are my buddies and I want them to have what I got."

To be honest, I live to do just that. Preaching the Gospel has been the focus of my life. I live to tell the world what I told Roscoe—the simple message of the Gospel, "the power of God unto salvation," and it still works.

Thanks, Coach, for teaching me to have a passion for the souls of men.

• • • •

Perhaps the highlights of my ministry years came as I led groups to Russia in the early 1990s. The wall had collapsed, and Americans were openly traveling to the former Soviet Union.

I remember the Cold War with all its threats of nuclear war. As a young boy in elementary school, I recall climbing under our desks in our "nuke" drills.

My most vivid memory of verbal threats came when the Soviet premier, Nikita Khrushchev, came to New York City to give a speech to the United Nations General Assembly. In a moment of anger, Khrushchev took off his shoe and pounded it on the UN table, blurting, "We will bury your grandchildren in Communism!"

That threat was chilling to a 9 year-old-boy. Russia and the USA became bitter enemies. Fidel Castro led Cuba into Communism just ninety miles off our coast. The USA discovered nuclear warheads from Russia in Cuba, which brought us to the brink of nuclear war. The Olympics even became a battleground, as athletes from the USA and the Soviet Union demonstrated their nationalism. Finally, the USA and Russia competed in sending rockets and men into space.

As a boy, I wanted to win every encounter with the Soviets. The Communists threatened my freedoms, and I had a bitter spirit toward them. So whether it was Olympic competition, space, nuclear arms race, or chess, I wanted to win! I did not want the prophecy of Khrushchev to come true.

In 1992, I couldn't believe that I was on a voyage to Russia! Times had truly changed. Our destination was Samara, the third largest city in Russia. This former "secret" city was the aerospace capital of Russia. Nestled on the Volga River, Samara had a population of over two-million people. The city had only one hotel and one Baptist church!

I had recruited a strong NCAA Division I men's basketball team. We were scheduled to play in an international tournament in Samara. The city dispatched a new jetliner to fly to Moscow, meet us, and fly us into Samara. I learned later that we were the first Americans to visit Samara in 70 years!

During our chartered flight from Moscow to Samara, the organizers came back to my seat and asked if I'd like to visit the cockpit. As I entered the cockpit, the co-captain got out of his seat and motioned for me to sit at the controls.

Wow! I couldn't believe it. I was sitting in the cockpit of a Russian military jet and flying in Russian airspace. When the captain motioned for me to take hold of the controls, my mind raced back to the nuclear drills in elementary school. The moment was surreal.

I had fun playing the role of pilot. I took a couple of dips and banked the plane sharply a few times. The players were slightly unsettled, but I was like a little boy playing Tom Cruise.

On our second day in Samara, the mayor of the city sent for our delegation. This abrupt visit to City Hall was unplanned, and I was a little concerned.

When our team walked into a big auditorium, we were greeted by hundreds of citizens, as well as television crews and journalists. When the mayor and his aides walked into the room, they invited me to the platform. The mayor was very gracious in his remarks, welcoming us and mentioning that we were the first Americans to visit Samara in over 70 years. He proceeded to present me with a huge piece of silver to take to my wife, who could not make the trip.

I was then asked to give a response. What could I say? How could I tell them about our real purpose in visiting Russia?

I responded by pulling off my shoe and pounding on the table like Khrushchev in New York City. I pounded my shoe for a couple of minutes. The Russians began to smile and my team began to sweat. They never knew about the threatening remarks at the United Nations. I could tell the team was thinking about their possible banishment to Siberia.

145

When I felt I had made my point, I began my speech.

"I remember your premier coming to the USA and saying he would bury our grandchildren in Communism," I began.

"Well, we are those grandchildren. It is Stalin and Lenin who are dead. Khrushchev is also dead and Communism is dying. But we have come to Russia to tell you about Jesus Christ. He was the Son of God, Who came into the world, lived a perfect life, died on the cross, and was buried. But, three days later, He walked out of the grave, and He is alive forever."

I was stunned as the Russians stood to their feet in an ovation.

"We're here to tell you we love you and God loves you," I continued. "You can also have eternal life in Heaven, if you repent of your sins, trust Jesus Christ and what He did for you on the cross, and commit your life to Him. That's why we are in Samara."

I sat down. To see how open and receptive those Russians were to the Gospel was an awesome sight.

That evening over six-thousand Russians packed inside the local basketball arena to watch the USA take on the Russians. After a great first half, we gave a couple of testimonies, and Joe Jordan preached the Gospel to the crowd, who listened intently. Since the halftime lasted only 15 minutes, Joe invited the spectators to stay in their seats until after the game, when he would share more about Jesus. We also promised to give everyone who stayed a Bible.

After the game, I was stunned to see every Russian remain glued to their seats. No one moved! Joe gave another powerful, clear presentation of the Gospel. Thousands received Christ, and everyone got a Bible as they exited. God touched all of our hearts as we watched Russians take possession of the Word of God, which was never seen outside the Russian church for 70 years.

We were blessed to work with the Baptist church in the follow-up of converts. Though they were uneducated in evangelism—a practice that was illegal for 70 years—those believers knew how to teach the Bible. For two weeks, we played games, preached the Gospel, worshipped at the Baptist church, and distributed Bibles in a country that I came to love.

Many times I have heard Joe Jordan repeat that the only two things on earth that are eternal are the Word of God and the souls of men. Thanks to my mentor, Bruce Foster, I found that investing my life in the pursuit of God's Word and lost souls would result in eternal rewards.

• • • •

In 1979, after we won our first national championship at TTU, a special event happened in our gymnasium. Ronald Reagan, who became a candidate for President of the United States, announced a campaign stop in Chattanooga. Because his campaign team wanted to identify him with the "religious right," they decided to make a major campaign speech on our campus.

Prior to his arrival, the Secret Service did background checks on all of our gym staff. This visit was greatly anticipated and hyped.

I remember the White House press corps and major media correspondents arriving the day of the event. Thousands gathered in our gym, as the band greeted Mr. Reagan, who gave his usual rousing speech. Reagan was such a great communicator.

Knowing the place of his exit, I positioned myself with our staff at the rear exit of our gymnasium. As I waited for senators and our mayor to file out the door, I was positioned to say farewell to Mr. Reagan.

Finally, surrounded by Secret Service agents, he approached me standing at the exit. I reached out my hand to him and froze in that moment of time. I have been in the presence of many great coaches, athletes, and preachers, but never speechless or intimidated.

"Mr. Reagan, I used to watch you on GE Theater," I blurted. Suddenly a surge of embarrassment rushed through my body. "What was that?" I thought. The old GE Theater television show Ronald Reagan hosted was barely a memory. For my young staff standing beside me, it had to be a joke, because Mr. Reagan began to laugh.

"Son," he said. "You don't look that old." And with that, he was whisked into the waiting limousine.

"GE Theater?" one of my staff members asked. "What does that have to do with the world of politics?"

Two years later, while on vacation, I took my family to visit Washington. We got a VIP tour of the White House. After the tour, we were headed to the car.

"Dad, wait a minute," Rhonda blurted out. "We're leaving and you didn't introduce me to President Reagan."

"President Reagan? You can't just go into the White House and expect to meet the President," I said.

"But, Dad, you know him. You have talked to him. He visited you in the gym."

That day I tried, unsuccessfully, to explain to my 8 year-old-daughter that you can know someone and not really know them.

That night I went to sleep wondering how many people know Jesus Christ but have no relationship with Him. Many know a lot of facts about Him but do not, in reality, know Him. I was reminded of the words of Jesus, who said, "In that day I will say unto, depart from me, you workers of iniquity. For I never knew you."

Although we did meet once, I know that President Reagan never really knew me,. I proudly display a picture of President Reagan in my office. Beside the picture is a letter I received in 1981 from President Reagan—a letter of congratulations that he sent after we won our second NCCAA national championship title. My passion is to present Jesus Christ to people in such a way that they don't have a casual acquaintance, but a personal and intimate relationship with Him.

REFLECTIONS ON WINNING

CHAPTER 14

BORN TO COACH

I was born to coach! Coaching is more than putting a whistle around your neck, screaming at a group of guys, berating officials, and playing ego games with students, fans, and media.

Pat Summitt, head coach of the University of Tennessee Lady Vols and the winningest Division I coach in NCAA history, says that coaching is <u>teaching</u>. Mike Krzyzewski, men's coach at Duke says, "I don't look at myself as a coach. I look at myself as a <u>leader</u>." Coaching is an opportunity to <u>mentor</u>—being a <u>role model</u> and seeking to impact young people. Coaching means fostering relationships with youths in order to share positive life skills.

These thoughts are similar to my philosophy. Before I began my coaching career, I struggled with how to balance my calling to preach with coaching. I knew that I was a preacher who happened to coach and never wanted to be known as a coach who happened to preach.

Therefore, I developed my three-pronged philosophy.

1.   Coaching is a ministry.
2.   Coaching is a means to an end.
3.   Coaching is a mode to attaining goals.

From the very beginning, I justified my career in coaching as a ministry. I used sports as a platform. The visibility and publicity provided opportunities to share my faith. Coaching became a means to mentor young men, to publicly promote the person of Jesus Christ, and to project an image to impact young people with the principles of God's Word. I used my role as coach to widen my sphere of influence as a preacher. Being a coach has allowed me to meet influential people, make national news, be on television, and use my influence in church circles around the country.

My college coaching career propelled me into the national limelight. The success was captured week after week in local newspapers and didn't stop there! In 1984, The *USA TODAY*, a publication with national circulation in the millions, printed a three-column article about me. I had television interviews and a nationally telecasted game. President Ronald Reagan sent a letter of congratulations after a national championship. The Tennessee State Senate adopted resolutions several times, acknowledging the success of our Tennessee Temple program. I received congratulatory letters from both U.S. Senators from Tennessee, the Third District U.S. Congressman, the Governor of Tennessee, and the Mayor of Chattanooga.

The attention resulted in hundreds of invitations to speak to youth groups, churches, camps, banquets, and Christian schools all over the United States. This was the vehicle that God used to allow me to preach the Gospel on a national level. Sports truly was a means to an end!

However, I cannot deny that I enjoyed the ride! With solid recruiting, implementing a sensible philosophy and marketing a good program, our staff rode to the top of the mountain. In 1984, we were nationally ranked above all Christian colleges.

People often ask me my greatest moment in coaching. Eight of our 10 years, TTU was in the Final Four of the National Christian College Athletic Association national tournament. Six times, we played in the championship game. Four times, our teams won the NCCAA national championship. Our 10 year record was unmatched by any Christian college in the USA. There were so many great moments.

I remember my first year of coaching. Actually, the record was not bad, but our team never achieved as we planned. We finished 17–12, but the season was filled with frustrations. We had a couple of players who gave our coaching staff a lot of problems. They were very moody, selfish, and divided our team through defiance.

I remember coming into the dressing room after our final game. I knew I would not have these two guys back. I promised the team that night that I would go out and recruit so that they would be playing for a championship and be proud to be a Crusader.

Danny Smith and Victor Hazard were great people recruited by Coach Foster. Both were high school standouts who had all-state credentials. Danny went to Purdue University on a football scholarship. He was all-state in two sports in Indiana. Victor, a 6'7" African-American from Rhode Island, was a great outside shooter.

After his freshman year at Purdue, Danny transferred to Temple to study for the ministry. He was a 6'1" guard who was strong and had a nose for the ball. He had so much confidence in his abilities that he always wanted the ball when the game was on the line. His biggest problem was that he detested coming out of a game. Defensively,

155

Danny always guarded our opponent's best guard. I can remember three games that Danny won for Temple with field goals on our last possession.

Victor was also talented, but in a different way. Although Danny could score, he was most valuable to us as a defensive stopper. Victor seemed to enjoy only one end of the court! I never saw a 6'7" player with greater range. When Victor played, we did not have a three-point line. If we had, I am sure he would have averaged well over 20 points-per-game. How do you guard a 6'7" guy who shot the ball from 20 to 24 feet with deadly precision?

These guys were our great leaders. They were not only leaders on the court but also on the campus and in the classroom. Danny was a straight-A student. Victor made good grades, but his greatest asset was his personality on campus. Neither caused us any problems. Danny won the national Murchison Award, which was given to the Christian athlete who excelled in basketball, in the classroom, and in spiritual leadership.

I remember telling an opposing coach one night before the game, "You see that guy (pointing to Smith)? "He's never made a B in the classroom." "I've got a lot of players like that!" The coach replied.

Danny and Victor helped us lay a foundation to build a championship program. Within 4 years, we won our first national championship; but unfortunately, both Danny and Victor graduated BEFORE we won a title. However, they paved the way for our success.

Today, they are both successful in life. Danny went on to Dallas Theological Seminary and Georgia Medical School. He is a pulmonologist and practices medicine in Chattanooga. Victor is a vice-president of the University of Kentucky in Lexington. The foundation of a championship team begins with people with character and commitment.

When a person gets a college coaching job, there are two things that are vital. First, you must build a foundation for a championship program. Once you have built a championship program, maintaining that program is probably more difficult.

Laying the foundation is easy, especially when the program has never won a championship. If a school has never been to the top, you cannot fail. No one knows what to expect. Administrators do not give coaches any formulas for making it happen.

As I began my career as a head coach, I outlined six things that I felt were my priorities to building a championship program:

1. Vision
2. Staff
3. Resources
4. Talent
5. Relationships
6. Work ethic

These six building blocks became the foundation for guiding me as I built a championship program.

VISION. Every coach has to have a vision for his program. He has to know where he wants to go. He has to be purpose-driven, goal-oriented, and focused. Successful coaches make game plans for each game. Vision is a statement of where you want to go and developing a game plan to get there.

STAFF. Coaches who win are those who surround themselves with talented people whose gifts complement the head coach's. The head coach must select people whose strengths can neutralize his own weaknesses. A successful head coach delegates responsibilities, utilizing the strengths of his staff and giving them the freedom to function without controlling their efforts. Leadership is guiding a staff to stay focused on the larger picture, instead of being enamored with their gifts and personal agendas. A head coach should never feel threatened by the staff's success.

In selecting a competent staff, I looked for three basic traits:

1. Respect. I was always taught to respect elders; however, respect is not measured by age, but by position. People who do not respect those in authority are not trustworthy.

2. Loyalty. Loyalty is one of my highest values in a staff member. Everyone can be loyal. People who are disloyal lack character, are selfish, and tend to be ego-driven. Blind loyalty also poses a danger. A leader must be ethical, honest, and credible. To such a leader, staff is obligated to be loyal.

3. Passion. People must share the passion of their leader. They must see the big picture and work hard to make the vision a reality. A staff who works together with passion to accomplish the vision will achieve success.

RESOURCES. To be successful at the collegiate level, a coach must have resources to build and maintain a championship team. Finances must be available to provide for scholarships, salaries, recruiting, apparel, and equipment. Schools that do not provide funding should not have high expectations for success. Resources provide assurance and security to coaches that the school administration is serious about competing.

TALENT. Recruiting talent is the key to success! Coaches take a lot of unwarranted credit. The team with the best talent usually wins the championship. If a coach can mold, manage, and motivate a team, he can win games without a lot of knowledge of Xs and Os; provided, he has extraordinary players. However, a great coach who knows the game, breaks down the game, and teaches the game will be mediocre at best with inferior talent. People should refrain from heaping praise on coaches who have superior talent. If a coach has an all-state player on a high school team or an All-American on a college team, then HE SHOULD WIN!

I will be the first to admit, after being named as the National Coach of the Year twice, that without talented players, we would have never won a championship. Talent builds resumes for coaches. Superior talent gives coaches glowing won-lost records. Players deserve all the recognition, because they are the ones playing the game—defending, rebounding, and scoring the buckets. Successful coaches who are not ego-driven recognize this fact.

RELATIONSHIPS. To build and maintain a championship program, a coach has to build good relationships. He has to be a people person. Perhaps one of the most misunderstood people in college basketball is Bobby Knight. The media portrays him as an out-of-control bear, who intimidates everyone around him. The truth about Bobby Knight is that he chooses the people with whom he wants to build such relationships. He has a distaste for the media and offends many people; yet, if you interviewed players and their parents, you would find a group of people who would take a bullet for him. He is loyal, honest, and trustworthy.

Successful coaching must be built on relationships with peers, faculty and administration, the student body, donors and influential people, and the parents of potential recruits. Unlike Knight, building solid relationships with the media in the early stages of your career is also critical.

WORK ETHIC. A coach may lack people skills, knowledge of the game, resources, and talent, but he has no excuse for not working hard. Championship coaches stay up late and rise early. They love to work and love the work they do. To be a winning coach, a person has to be committed to hard work.

When a coach has a solid understanding of why he does what he does, is willing to make a commitment to his profession, and then works hard to achieve his vision, he puts himself in a position to be a champion. The ingredients for a championship program include having a vision, surrounding oneself with people who share this vision, and finding and mentoring a team of guys willing to commit to the vision.

CHAPTER 15

KEYS TO WINNING

People have asked me through the years what are the keys to winning. How does a coach communicate to young athletes the ingredients to becoming a champion? In individual sports, such as wrestling, golf, tennis, or track, they are simpler to identify. Basically, becoming a champion in individual sports depends upon three things:

1. Desire
2. Discipline
3. Determination

DESIRE. Desire means the athlete "wants" to be a champion. Parents and coaches may motivate an athlete, but he must "want" to become better than good. Such desire will carry the athlete when adversity strikes. Desire drives the athlete to finish when he is tempted to quit. Without a strong desire, the athlete will be content to accept mediocrity. No one can instill that "want to" in an athlete; it must come from within. He must be driven to succeed.

DISCIPLINE. Discipline means blocking out all distractions and staying focused on one's stated goals. Once an athlete defines his objective, discipline means abstaining from everything that opposes success. He must commit to time, energy, and effort. Discipline means working out alone, often while others are at ease. Discipline requires going to the gym alone and shooting 500 shots, hitting 500 golf balls on the practice course, or analyzing and studying ways to improve.

DETERMINATION. Determination is overcoming all obstacles and pressing on to achieve success. Determination toughens in the face of adversity, keeps a refuse-to-lose mind-set, and never compromises energy and effort. This type of mental toughness drives one to excel when the body craves quitting.

Gerald Wilkins was a great basketball player at the University of Tennessee-Chattanooga. His brother, Dominique, was an all-star NBA player. Gerald was a quick, wiry, slashing defensive college player. I never thought Gerald would play long in the NBA, but Gerald spent 13 years in the league, mostly with the New York Knicks. He averaged over 10 points-per-game in those 13 years but was mostly a defensive stopper. A 6'6" guard, Gerald guarded Michael Jordan on numerous occasions. I always wondered how Gerald stayed in the league so long. He was good but not great; and yet, he enjoyed a wonderful NBA career.

One day, I heard that Gerald was working out at the Chattanooga Salvation Army gymnasium. I decided to go see Gerald work out. He had a personal trainer by the name of Randy Webb. Randy was well known in Chattanooga for his ability to work with athletes.

When I walked into the gym, I was shocked! Randy was putting Gerald through a rigorous workout. They were in the gym alone. Sweat was pouring off Gerald's body. I watched with fascination as this trainer drove Gerald hard, almost to the limits of physical exhaustion. I later learned that this was a four-hour session. They were totally oblivious to the fact that I stood at the other end of the gym.

Now I knew why Gerald has almost zero body fat. I knew why he was able to check Michael Jordan effectively. I realized why this average player was able to have such a long career in the NBA. He had desire, discipline, and determination. While other NBA stars were on the beach, Gerald was in the gym. Not until a young athlete has this kind of drive can he reach and sustain his maximum potential.

Young athletes need to learn from Gerald Wilkins the secret of becoming a champion!

Team sports demand the following intangible keys to success:

1. Understanding
2. Sacrifice
3. Loyalty

UNDERSTANDING. A successful team is comprised of individuals blended together who understand their role and the true meaning of a team concept. The key is to understand your role. There is absolutely nothing democratic about the concept of team.

EVERYONE IS NOT EQUAl. (Sacrifice and Loyalty). On a basketball court, the team has one point guard or captain. A presidential cabinet has designated individual roles, but every person is accountable to someone. Most churches have a pastoral team but only ONE senior pastor. To become successful on a team, every player must understand his role and perform that role for the good of the team.

CHAPTER 16

LOSING AT OUR OWN GAME

I have many concerns about the current condition of U.S. basketball. Things have changed drastically, and we are paying a price as the game deteriorates.

Dr. Naismith would be appalled to see the game today. While the athletes are bigger, quicker, and more talented, the quality of the game has been prostituted. We invented the game but have "outsourced" the fundamentals.

In 1986, I began to take teams overseas. We conducted clinics for coaches, played games against foreign competition, and held camps to teach basic skills. SCORE International was not the first ministry to do this. Teaching the game overseas has been done for approximately half a century.

During the Olympics, the USA always had a lock on the gold medal, at least until Russia emerged. Foreign teams began to use older, more experienced players to occasionally defeat our better college all-star teams. However, foreign teams were advancing so fast that the USA basketball federation decided to send an NBA "Dream Team" to compete in the Barcelona Olympics. Once again, the USA established itself as the dominant basketball power in the world with Michael Jordan, Magic Johnson, Charles Barkley, David Robinson, and others.

Meanwhile, those foreign teams continued to improve at a fast pace. NBA teams began to draft young talent from overseas. The emergence of such players as Hakeem Olajuan, Dikembe Mutumbo, Tony Parker, Manu Ginonobli, and Tim Duncan give us a reality check. Basketball is no longer just an American sport, and we no longer dominate.

Our recent losses in international competition using NBA players proves most embarrassing of all. In 2003, Argentina won the World Championship in Indianapolis, putting USA basketball in a frenzy. Then they won the gold medal in Athens at the 2004 Olympics.

So, what has happened?

I believe there are several explanations. I want to list four reasons why I believe we are losing ground:

1. Neglect of fundamentals
2. Lack of intensity on defense and rebounding
3. Too much emphasis on individual play
4. Infusion of large amounts of money

NEGLECT OF FUNDMENTALS. One of the things we taught foreign coaches and players was how to play the game fundamentally. We emphasized ball handling, passing, shooting, pick and rolls, and rebounding. Today, coaches place very little emphasis on basic skills.

Coaches have neglected to TEACH THE GAME. We have allowed players to concentrate on things that will not build their total game. High school practice no longer features skill drills. As a result, shooting percentages, ball handling (notice how players today carry the ball), and passing have deteriorated. We see today's players dribbling between their legs, behind the back, and picking up the dribble without looking to pass. While some of these things may be necessary at times, they encourage too many turnovers.

Meanwhile, international players have mastered "our" fundamentals, working hard on their skills. International coaches have become very technical and demanding in their instruction and insist that their players polish techniques.

I know many do not agree with my observations, but the World Baseball Classic is another prime example. The Japanese won the inaugural event while the USA did not even advance to the semifinals. Americans invented baseball also. Players from the Far East and Latin countries focus on the execution of fundamental skills—fielding, bunting, hitting behind runners on base, and executing a good running game to advance men on base. The point is simple: we are losing in international basketball and baseball competition because of fundamental inferiority. We are no longer the BEST in the world!

LACK OF INTENSITY ON DEFENSE AND REBOUNDING.

Most players do not know how to play defense. Players are allowed to play at less than maximum. Practice sessions are not intense. Defensive principles are not explained, demonstrated, or emphasized. Players rest on the defensive end, where past players would turn-it-up a notch. Few teams practice boxing out and other rebounding drills. Players no longer follow shots but stand, admire, and forfeit the ball on an errant field goal attempt. Sadly, we see coaches practice players without a timed practice schedule, with little teaching, and too much scrimmaging.

For this reason, the Argentines are taking the game to our NBA players. They play hard defense, rebound, and play to the maximum of their potential.

TOO MUCH EMPHASIS ON INDIVIDUAL PLAY. Everyone who studies international teams knows that they play extremely well together. Very little attention is given to one player. Rather, their style is team-focused. In the USA, our half court offenses feature too much dribbling, too little passing, and not enough movement without the ball. Sure, we can see Kobe Bryant score 81 points, Allen Iverson can jack up 30 shots in a game, and Tracy McGrady may get 35 points on a given night, but their teams continue to lose! That is why the NBA has so many BAD teams. The San Antonio Spurs and Detroit Pistons are an exception.

Michael Jordan is arguably the greatest player to ever play basketball. Why was he great? Because he made everyone around him better. He played on both ends of the floor. He was a team player and carried his teams to six world championships.

Recently, I watched a high school team with a 6'10" player. The team featured three guards who could shoot. Sadly, they did too much. None of the guards averaged more than two assists a game. Meanwhile, the 6'10" player led the team in three-point-shooting percentage. What does that say? Guards are not passing, but selfishly looking to shoot. Sadly, all three guards will someday play college basketball but will not have a 6'10" teammate. They will read in the papers about the 6'10", but they will know that it is too late. They will realize that they could have been better all-around players if they had seen on the floor what thousands saw in the stands. For some reason, the coaches on the bench never saw it either.

INFUSION OF LARGE AMOUNTS OF MONEY. There is so much emphasis on money. Everything seems driven by the dollar. Huge professional contracts, endorsements, agents, and marketing have escalated sports to a level of absurdity. Frankly, athletes consider themselves entertainers and are grossly overpaid. Driven by unhealthy egos, many are not prepared to handle such huge amounts of money; therefore, they engage in unhealthy lifestyles and become poor role models to the youth who look up to them.

This tendency begins in the early teen years of an athlete. Players with talent and/or size become targets of early recruiting. They receive funding from shoe companies. AAU coaches become like vultures, hoping to seize players and parents for selfish gain. Many coaches are untrained. These coaches promise parents scholarships as they expose players to scouts. Some even look beyond to the NBA.

Parents are easy targets. They get consumed by the attention, financial rewards, and ego. They routinely miss church on Sunday to get their child to an AAU event in the summer. After all, they feel their star athlete has to play a lot to receive the attention and exposure to get the best deal from the biggest name. Sadly, the athlete gets prostituted by a host of pimps who rarely considers their spiritual, social, and educational welfare.

This pattern has devastated the development of American athletes. Fundamentals and team concept are secondary to showcasing the individual skills of a prospect. This explains why our USA teams can no longer beat the Argentines, who only discovered basketball 30 years ago. They can pick and roll, pass, and shoot with facility. Although they are not good at dunking, dribbling between the legs, or taking a defender one-on-one, they can beat a group of Americans at their "own" game.

Some will say that our best players do not commit to play in international competition, which is a valid and correct argument. International competition does not have the financial pay-off. Some of our more talented athletes refuse to represent their country in international competition for these financial reasons.

REFLECTIONS ON MINISTRY

CHAPTER 17

PANGS OF MINISTRY

Many want to begin a ministry and be where we are today. They expect to start where we are now. They see the success, the blessings, the hand of God, and they want the same NOW!

It is so much easier to join a ministry or take over a work. Plowing is a lot tougher than gathering the harvest. Working on a farm conditioned me for ministry. I know what it means to break "new ground" behind a mule. I have plowed all day long; I have sowed seeds and hoed weeds; I have watered and reaped the harvest.

When God cast a vision in my heart to start SCORE International, it was frightening. Pat and I were alone, with no resources, support, or help. I had a good job, successful coaching career, and financial stability. I walked away from a steady income to a venture without any promise of support. God planted the vision in my heart, but it still took a leap of faith.

Sports–missions ministry was unique in the South. No one else was doing it in our region of the country. I didn't copy from anyone or steal someone's ideas. I was not mentored by anyone or taught. Pat and I just walked in obedience to the call.

I hear people talk about the TEAM concept of ministry, but I realized that my wife and I WERE the team. I wouldn't have it any other way! Because Pat and I had to look to God for every need, we had to walk in faith every week to experience His goodness and grace. We couldn't get opinions from others; we had to hear from our Father.

Today, people see properties, buses, buildings, large staff, and big budgets. They see the assets of SCORE International. They hear about the large numbers. They know we are based in multiple countries. They can add it all up in their heads. What they do not see are the sacrifices and struggles to get here:

- Initial years of meager budgets
- Ten years having our office in our home
- Eleven years of laboring ALONE
- Twelve years of ministry with only ten supporting churches

We did not get to where we are today easily. People covet what we have today but do not see the sleepless nights, the fears, the pressures, and the anxieties. It was just like preseason—two-a-days in the hot sun. I considered quitting but kept running—I'm glad I did.

The first person to support us monthly was Bea Davis, a retired Baptist Mid-Missions missionary. She was an unlikely donor, but she sent $10 per month for years. Antioch Baptist Church in Ona, West Virginia, was our first supporting church. After these initial supporters, the support began to flow consistently.

Today, SCORE International has a multi-million dollar budget. We have a Board of Directors with twenty people serving. We have assets and staffs in three countries. We have two Missions Training Centers, three orphanages, a Dental/Medical clinic, a bi-lingual institute, numerous vehicles, and land. We have also partnered with a Foundation to build a sports complex and Bible college.

God has given us a staff of over seventy people. Our home office is in Chattanooga. We have great workers, with a good balance of Americans and nationals. God's good hand and the hearts and hands of many volunteers and staff have made the work a success.

Each year we take over three-thousand people overseas. The numbers steadily increase annually. Our ministry facilitates short term mission trips, plants churches, helps national pastors and missionaries, and impacts the people we take overseas.

At what point did the success begin? I would have to say that SCORE International has experienced success today because of the work I began in 1968. But you say, 1968? I thought SCORE International began in 1985. And, if you labored alone for 11 years, didn't the success begin in 1996? No! We are enjoying God's blessings today, because almost forty years before SCORE International was founded, I was traveling all over the USA meeting pastors, preaching in churches, and meeting people. SCORE International is enjoying the fruit of 40 years of preparation, praying, plowing, and preaching. I understand Moses. No significant work for God was ever birthed to full adulthood. That's why adopting a ministry is easier than give birth to one. However, founding a ministry and learning to lean alone on the One who cast the vision makes the effort rewarding.

People often ask me, when will you retire? My answer is, why? I enjoy my ministry. I love to preach. I live to make a significant impact on others. I want to have a meaningful work for God. I have NEVER planned to quit. Oh, I may turn it all over to someone else in the future, but I plan to stay active in the work as long as I am able.

If you check my resume, one thing will be very obvious to you. I DO NOT MOVE MUCH. Since Pat and I married, we have lived in only two cities. I was with Tennessee Temple for 15 years and have been with SCORE International for 21 years. During those years, I have gained a lot of experience as a television commentator, NBA speaker, pastoral staff, coach, preacher, and missionary. Despite this versatility, I never jumped around, moved, or lost my focus. I have discovered that building a ministry takes a long term commitment. You cannot quit, resign, turn back, or slow down. I never needed motivation, pep talks, or seminars. God gave me His Word, led me by His Spirit, and cast a vision for ministry in my heart.

When my time expires, I will still say that I have always enjoyed ministry. The tough times were only challenges. Winning has always been about being prepared when opportunity arises, in spite of the challenges and adverse circumstances. The opponent may throw a full-court press at us, but we can advance up the court and score if we have a good scouting report and game plan. After all, we are on the winning side!

• • • •

I have experienced many highs and lows in ministry. Through it all, I can say that the Lord has given me strength, assurance, and wisdom. My ministry has taken me to some great mountaintops.

The experience of pastoring the church in Alabama was great for me and my young family. Traveling across the USA for Word of Life, preaching at Superbowls and in some of America's greatest basketball arenas, I have seen thousands of teenagers trust Christ. This has always kept me on the firing line. The NBA arenas included the home of the Orlando Magic, Miami Heat, Cleveland Cavaliers, Philadelphia 76ers, Washington Wizards, Atlanta Hawks, and New Jersey Nets. God gifted me to preach to thousands of teens, down on the court, after NBA games. Speaking at Operation Nightmares attracted thousands of teens. I have driven hearses with coffins across the Midwestern states and preached to kids at the Scaremares. We scared the devil out of many teens.

I have preached in some of America's greatest Baptist churches. I have been privileged to personally know a lot of leading pastors in our country. Dr. Jerry Falwell has been especially kind to me.

With all of its joys and successes, ministry has also had its downside. I have walked through a lot of valleys. I have often been hurt, wounded, and disappointed. I have twice gone through valleys, out of which I could not climb.

For 10 years I enjoyed my ministry at the Calvary Baptist Church in Chattanooga. Pastor Kelton Williams was extremely kind, gracious and generous to me. We became good friends. He allowed me a lot of freedom, taught me how to play and enjoy the game of golf, and gave me opportunities to serve the Lord as his assistant pastor. We experienced great days of ministry, as the church drew almost six-hundred regular attendees to weekly services. The church prospered financially, and we had great Spirit-filled services.

Unfortunately, we encountered problems as the devil invaded our work. Pastor Williams was asked to resign as the result of those problems. Many unanswered questions remained, which have never been fully resolved.

I was asked by the deacons to be the interim pastor. After some days of prayer, I agreed to do the work, only if I would be the interim PASTOR, not just a figure to fill the pulpit. I soon learned that being interim pastor is a no-win situation. An interim pastor is a preacher with a lot of RESPONSIBILITY but no AUTHORITY. If a man does well in this position, people in the pew begin to campaign for the interim to become the pastor.

After eleven months, I realized I had a problem. Actually, I learned I WAS THE PROBLEM! No candidate received a 75 percent vote. A large number of people wanted me, so I had to resign and get out of the way. In October 2000, I resigned and left the church. A few months later, Calvary Baptist Church called Steve Roberson as their pastor.

I was happy because Steve was a person I wanted there all the time. Several deacons pushed for his candidacy, but a power play by a few of the influential deacons and several member of the search committee thwarted his coming. They wanted an older man, in the mold of Brother Kelton. They wanted the church to keep the status quo and opposed the pastor traveling to preach in other places, which is what Steve Roberson and I have always done.

The most disappointing aspect for me was to deal with the bitterness some people had toward me. Steve invited me back to Calvary in October 2001. I was honored to walk into the pulpit 1 year after my resignation. I was honored to receive a standing ovation by the church I had served for ten years. I stood there with tears, one month after the terrorist strike in New York City on September 11. In spite of the showing of love and support, I later learned that two families left the church that day because I preached. I also found out that a few people, who were close to those powerful people who left, had bitter feelings toward me.

The result has been devastating in many ways. I have NEVER been invited back! I have not been invited by the pastor for more than 6 years to preach to the people whom I still love. This attack has been hurtful to my family, but I am proud to say that we have been healed by the worship, expository preaching, and fellowship of friends in our new church. I am so thankful that my family has never been disillusioned, distracted, or disappointed enough to blame God, quit church, or hold animosity toward other believers.

Difficulties in ministry will come. Brothers in Christ will have differences. The result has been devastating to many families. I have seen children give up, quit, and drop out simply because of the perceived carnal treatment of their parents in ministry. In His blessing, God has spared Pat and me from that anguish. I believe the depth of spiritual commitment by Robyn and Rhonda is the reason for their strength. However, a lot of credit must be given to Pat because of her discernment and perception of our real enemy.

• • • •

I have faced another battle in the Dominican Republic. My sister, her husband, his niece, and her husband raised support to go to the Dominican Republic and plant a church in San Pedro de Macoris. They were SCORE International missionaries; however, soon after they got their support, my sister's son-in-law felt led to resign SCORE because his home church began a mission organization. He desired to become one of their first missionaries. To keep unity and peace in the family, my sister and her husband also resigned SCORE to form a team under the umbrella of the church to do the work in San Pedro.

I have never had a problem with that decision. To be honest, I hated to see them leave SCORE because I was behind such a project and wanted to support it. Their ministry was only 10 MILES away from our work in the Dominican Republic. I did not want the duplication of our ministry. Two things concerned me. One was our identity as a sports–missions ministry, hosting sports teams from the USA to use sports as a evangelistic tool. Second, I did not want to see the duplication of our ministry of hosting short-term missions groups that close to our hotel. Although we had an agreement not compete against each other's purpose statement, we have never reached an agreement on partnership.

I can partner with Word of Life in the Dominican Republic, Southern Baptists in the Dominican Republic, and other independent Bible churches in the Dominican Republic—but am still isolated from my own family, 10 miles away in a foreign country. This really hurts me!

I can say this for certain: I refuse to allow ministry to interfere with my family relationship. We can agree not to partner in ministry, but when I am in the Dominican Republic, I will take my sister out to dinner. I refuse to allow any ministry disagreement to divide and destroy fellowship with those I truly love.

Ministry has hardships—many difficulties! The Apostle Paul encountered them. Every servant of God can recount many difficult situations in their quest to serve the Lord. Where there are people, you can always bet that there will be differences, but we can always agree to disagree and to do it the right way. Above all, our priority in every situation is that the name of Jesus be exalted, His Word proclaimed, and the message of the Gospel preached.

In spite of every effort by Satan to divide and conquer, I can truthfully say that the good times in ministry have outnumbered the hardships—it isn't even close. Therefore, I can boldly declare that we are "more than conquerors," victorious, and true winners. The Lord always knows how to encourage His team to press on, even when we can't see the victory. God is so faithful to strengthen and encourage us to press on, even when we desire to quit.

When I ran track in high school, I thought many times about quitting. Running the mile in competition was taxing on the body. It was a physically grueling race. At times, I thought I must be nuts. Why would I subject myself to such torture? Three-fourths through the race, I wanted to walk off the track. My heart was about to explode and my lungs were ready to collapse. Why was I doing this to myself? Just about the time my body convinced me to quit, I got my "second wind." When I saw the finish line and heard the cheers, I felt a burst of energy and new reason to finish the race. I refuse to believe the lies of my body. I never died on the track. I was a winner in spite of the physical torture.

God wants His servants to focus on finishing faithful. The pain will come from unsuspected places, but the joy of enduring through trying circumstances makes the victory worthwhile.

Whenever I have faced difficulties, God has faithfully and graciously placed me in the winner's circle in other venues of service. These ventures of victory have included preaching on national television in Mexico, Argentina, and Russia. I have enjoyed preaching to over six-thousand Russians at Samara. It was my privilege to preach to huge crowds in Argentina and Mexico as we traveled and played exhibition games against their national teams. God allowed me to speak to thousands upon thousands of Dominican boys at our baseball clinics, which featured Felipe Aloce, Kevin Malone, Don Gordon, Andy Phillips, and many other professional players and coaches. God gave me opportunities to preach His gospel in Rome, Paris, Mexico City, Prague, Buenos Aires, Moscow, San Jose, Montego Bay, Santo Domingo, San Juan, Lucerne, Amsterdam, and many other beautiful cities in the world.

If I could live my life over a hundred times, I would do things differently! I would study theology more intently. I would pray more earnestly. I would witness more passionately. I would worship more humbly. However, I can declare that the goodness and grace of God has followed me and sustained me. Jesus has been my greatest friend. True to His Word, He has never left me nor forsaken me.

When I bowed on my knees at the age of 18 and committed my life to Him; that was the most reasonable thing I ever did. That was the day

I began a journey into the winner's circle. That was the moment that life became most meaningful. The journey has taken me around the world to see the amazing power of the Gospel do its supernatural work.

CHAPTER 18

PARTNERSHIPS— GOD'S GAME PLAN

Most of my life I have been surrounded by people who seemed isolated from others. My early heritage as a Southern Baptist was very enlightening. I thought all Baptists were Southern Baptists. I did not realize until later how sheltered I was. Stepping outside the box in cooperative evangelistic efforts was rare. We had a "Cooperative Program," which meant we pooled our resources but always within the denomination.

Even today, many Southern Baptist churches, pastors, and leaders look only within their boundaries to do evangelistic, worldwide missions efforts. A theologically, biblically trained individual, whose faith corresponds with our Southern Baptist doctrines, has little opportunity to minister to or with most Southern Baptist congregations, even though those churches are autonomous. Although the International Mission Board has many gifted missionaries, mission agencies such as Christar, Word of Life, Operation Mobilization, Campus Crusade, AMG, Precept Ministries, New Tribes, and Wycliffe offer a multitude of opportunities to reach the unreached.

In the 1960s, many Southern Baptist congregations left the convention to become independent Baptists. The reason for their departure was liberalism in schools and seminaries, which affected a generation of students, pulpits, publications, and leadership. J. Frank Norris was a leader in the revolt of pastors across the South who chose to forsake the convention rather than stay and fight modernism. Thus, a movement was born. However, they became combative and legalistic. Sermons were laced with do's and don'ts and were focused on hair, dress, movies, music, etc. A person's relationship with God and spirituality was based on conformity to rules.

The independent Baptists were strong on evangelism, planting churches, missions, separation, faithfulness, and loyalty to the local church. The movement grew rapidly, becoming the largest Baptist congregations in most states. The Bible Baptist Fellowship, the Southwide Fellowship, the World Baptist Fellowship, and the General Association of Regular Baptists were founded as fellowships for the various groups of independent Baptists. Each fellowship founded colleges or Bible schools or affiliated with institutions already in existence.

Rarely did independent Baptist groups fellowship or cooperate with groups outside their boundaries. To join with evangelical churches or organizations beyond those boundaries was considered compromising and ecumenical. Under no circumstances did an independent Baptist church join with a Southern Baptist church in cooperative evangelism. They even refused to fellowship with others who did cross the lines. Thus, they practiced "secondary separation," an independent Baptist buzzword born in the 1970s.

I have survived both extremes with my Southern Baptist heritage and years in the independent Baptist movement. Both are terribly wrong to isolate themselves and minister inside the boxes and boundaries of institutions birthed by man.

Today, we are seeing an exciting emphasis on ministry partnerships. It has become evident that WE CANNOT CONTINUE to minister in our usual way and fulfill the Great Commission in our lifetime. One thing I learned as a coach is that we must make adjustments at halftime when we are losing. If my teams continue to do things the same way, without making adjustments, we will lose the game. The same is true in ministry. Our message NEVER changes, but if we fail to make adjustments in our methodology, we will never evangelize our culture!

We must never compromise our doctrinal positions. However, it is refreshing to move outside the box and cooperate in partnership with brethren of Biblical agreement to do global ministry. Partnering with other mission agencies, national missionaries, and churches brings added resources and talents to God's game plan.

God's game plan is really simple. You can see it in Matthew 28:19–20. God sends us to spread the good news of the Gospel to the entire world. We are to proclaim the Gospel, make disciples, and train converts to duplicate themselves. In Acts 1:8, we understand that we must be global as well as local. When we are filled with the Spirit of God, we will be energized, enabled, and engaged in missions simultaneously around the globe. We should not view this as a matter of "either/or" but "both/and".

Tasks can be accomplished in many ways as we engage in going, giving, and praying. However, the task can never be done without cooperative partnerships.

Through the years, SCORE International has partnered with Word of Life Fellowship, ABWE, Athletes in Action, Fellowship of Christian

Athletes, National Association of Christian Athletes, Without Borders, the International Mission Board, North America Mission Board, the International Baptist Network, Med-Send, and Global Focus. Believe me, these are just a few parachurch organizations.

We have also helped birth other sports ministries. The idea is not competition but cooperation. The world is too large and our sphere of influence is so limited. As we partner with others, we expand our borders and make Jesus famous. After all, our goal is to make His name known. We will fail if we simply make a name for ourselves; therefore, we find real significance in encouraging, edifying, and fellowshipping with partners in the ministry. In doing so, we will be able to corporately work toward the goal of evangelizing our generation. This IS God's game plan.

No denomination or parachurch ministry will ever accomplish world evangelism by working alone. God undoubtedly uses all of us to accomplish His game plan, but it is extremely rewarding to cross the boundaries and find the common biblical grounds to establish partnership. Personally, I have discovered that I can easily make that transition. Conservative Southern Baptists and independent Baptists, who have escaped the "spirit of legalism," are able to recognize their Biblical roots and heritage to find ways to partner in making Jesus famous and bringing people to Him.

Forty years of ministry have been a blast! They have gone by so very quickly. Beginning with the early days of jail ministry and street ministry, I have never doubted the call of God. Neither have I ever worried about a venue of service.

I have always believed that serving Christ can be fun. I have heard how some people felt compelled to go places and do things they did not enjoy. I can honestly say that God has gifted me, sent me, and guided me in areas of ministry that were compatible with my training and interests.

Most of my 40 years of ministry has been with teens and sports. I believe that I have the heart of a teenager and connect so well with them. Sports has been my avenue of service. Believing as Jerry Falwell, that teens all over the world speak the language of music and sports, my focus of ministry has been through sports.

Playing college sports gave me instant credibility and greater acceptance among teens. Years of college coaching opened thousands of doors to preach the Gospel to all ages. Those opportunities included the typical and traditional church meetings, Christian school chapels, youth camps, and evangelistic campaigns.

A piece of leather filled with air opened other doors, which included television and chapels for college and professional teams. Working as a color commentator for college basketball games on television was a huge break for me. I had the opportunity to meet many college coaches and had access to a large number of great college athletes. This broad spectrum of opportunities helped launch SCORE International to a higher level of credibility. I had so much fun doing those games that I hardly considered it work.

Conducting chapel for the NBA was another fantastic outreach for me. As a former coach, I related to NBA players. I never sought an autograph or a picture with the players. I was there to share the Word of God and make a spiritual impact. Sensitive to their needs, temptations, and goals, I believed my role was to expound the Word of God in a short, 15 minute, time frame, which would provide the spiritual direction and power to be a winner in life. Sharing the Word and praying with guys such as Mark Price (Cleveland), Mike Bibby (Sacramento), and Grant Hill (Orlando) just minutes before they played before fifteen-thousand fans and millions watching on television was simply a God thing.

"Chaplain, do you realize we are the only two guys in chapel who are over 30 years-old?" I once asked an NBA chaplain.

"Hey, Ron, we're the only two guys in here who are not multimillionaires," he retorted.

I was also able to do chapels at many college, NFL, and major league baseball teams.

One of my greatest moments in 1994 was going into the clubhouse of the visiting team prior to a major league baseball game at Fulton County Stadium in Atlanta. I drove through the gate with Kevin Malone (general manager of the Montreal Expos), John Zeller, Micah Hamrick, and the owner of the Expos. We parked underneath the stadium next to Bobby Cox, the great manager of the Atlanta Braves. I followed Kevin into the clubhouse as the Expos dressed and enjoyed a lavish spread of food, prior to taking the field.

I enjoyed seeing Felipe Alou, who was the manager of the Expos at that time. I reminded him that I was the teenage boy on a mission trip who visited him in his home in the Dominican Republic in 1963. We had a few minutes to visit before the Expos took the field.

Kevin Malone had a great professional career, which I helped launch. He came to Tennessee Temple from the University of Louisville to study in the seminary. I was the athletic director and gave him the role of assistant baseball coach under Coach John Zeller. Kevin did an awesome job; but since we did not have the funds to pay him, he agreed to coach if we paid his seminary school bill.

When Kevin left TTU, he began to work as a scout for the Minnesota Twins. During that time, Kevin successfully scouted teams and evaluated talent. During his tenure with the Twins, they won a World Series championship. Later, Kevin became general manager of the Expos, assistant general manager of the Baltimore Orioles, and ended his career in Los Angeles as the general manager of the Dodgers.

During his tenure with the Dodgers, Kevin invited me to spring training in Dodgertown, at Vero Beach, Florida. I had lunch with the Dodger executives prior to a game with the St Louis Cardinals. I also met Tommy Lasorda.

Before his retirement from baseball, I reminded Kevin that I was the one who gave him his first job in baseball.

"Yeah, I remember," he quipped. "I also remember that you never paid me anything."

Later, Kevin joined the Board of Directors of SCORE. He also became part owner of a Mercedes-Benz dealership with Eddie Murray, Hall of Fame player with the Baltimore Orioles. I did not realize at the time how significant the baseball connections of John Zeller and Kevin Malone would be for the SCORE international baseball ministry.

As I look back over my career in ministry, I realize that partnerships and relationships are God's way of accomplishing the greater agenda of God. I realize that I could never accomplish much as an independent servant, without being surrounded by a vast number of teammates. Our Sovereign Lord enlarges borders and broadens the scope of success, as He brings a multitude of generous, gifted people into our lives.

The most recent example of partnership in our ministry is with the Rawlings Foundation. Dr. Jerry Falwell contacted Herb Rawlings on my behalf. He told him of my desire to reach young Dominican men and make a spiritual impact on that culture. Herb is the son of Dr. John Rawlings. They have a family foundation, headed by George Rawlings and funded by the Rawlings Group. This family builds camps around the world. They desire to reach young people with the Gospel and give them Bible training.

Herb and I met in October 2005. I shared my heart with him. In November, Herb took a trip to the Dominican Republic to see our ministry. During that week, he saw the thousands of Dominican boys who attended our baseball clinics. He saw our vision. After returning to the states, he shared what he saw with his father and brothers.

God moved in their hearts to partner with us to build a sports complex and Bible college in the Dominican. The Rawlings Foundation will own the property, while SCORE will partner in the operations, administration, and ministry.

The property will include baseball fields, gymnasium, swimming pool, and dormitory for five-hundred Dominicans. With this sports complex, we will have sports camps, Bible camps, sports tournaments. We will also host high schools and colleges from the USA who will play against Dominican teams. The ultimate purpose is to evangelize and disciple the lost at this complex.

Herb has become a great friend as we partner together to share the Gospel. By partnering with friends like the Rawlings, we can expedite the work of God and pool our resources together, saving time, energy, and money. To duplicate ministry and re-invent wheels that already work proves senseless.

CHAPTER 19

RELATIONSHIPS EQUAL SUCCESS

No one ever achieves any measure of success without good mentors. Mentors are people who come alongside to share wisdom, experiences, encouragement, motivation, and information. People hungry to win look for pioneers to emulate who have blazed a trial of success.

God placed many people in my life. Many friends and relatives encouraged and guided me towards my dreams. To be honest, I never looked for them. I was too shy, proud, and maybe a bit stupid to believe I could do it myself. I could have never become a winner without a lot of teammates contributing to my success.

John Gamble was a businessman in Chattanooga. John was not a flashy guy. He owned a couple of service stations, known then as gasoline stations. John loved sports and athletes. He loved to hire guys who played basketball at Tennessee Temple College. John gave me a job at his Shell Oil station, where I worked third shift and made a little spending money.

God also used John to help me get my first fulltime job in ministry. As a deacon at Unity Baptist Church, John and his brother, James, recommended me to Pastor Billy Joe Smith. I became youth pastor. I leaned on John and James for help, advice, and wisdom.

I always wondered why John showed interest in me. He loved to help "his boys." There were a lot of us. Reg Cook, Jeff Heath, Lefty Glascock, Gary Terbeek. Through the years, there have been white guys and black guys. John just loved to mentor guys.

Mike Steele was one of the teens in my youth group at Unity. Mike was a popular athlete and good Christian kid with a lot of promise. Mike had a very tough home life, and John was there for him. John Gamble became a father figure for Mike. Forty years later, Mike still looks to John and honors him for his personal attention in his life.

Today, Mike is a bi-vocational pastor of a growing Southern Baptist Church and a politician, living in East Ridge, Tennessee. He married his high school sweetheart, Lynn, who was also in my youth group.

John has remained a loyal friend for many years. Because he cared for me, I was able to have a job and get a position on a local church staff. I was later ordained at Unity Baptist Church as a minister of the Gospel.

Carter McMasters is a 6'10" basketball player. For 3 years, I mentored Carter. We met for lunch and talked about basketball, education, and Christ—I love being involved in his life. I want to make a difference. Many people, including John Gamble, have made significant contributions to my life. Yes, it does take a village to shape a young life to become a winner.

People like John Gamble will never write a book. have a building named in their honor. They labor in o others find their way through life. They are the real h models and giants, whose only desire is to push othe thank God that John came into my life at a critical tim and Lefty, Reg, and Mike Steele.

• • • •

My greatest joy in ministry is to make an impact up Even though I began my coaching career at 21 years enjoyed my relationship with teens. When I retired f the age of 39, I was established as a youth speaker. Ev students in my ministry.

I seek to impact teens and mentor young people. explain why Paul Pittman, Todd Adkins, April and Ke many others, wanted me to do their wedding ceremor

I was warmed by the invitation of Carter McN mentor. Carter, a 6'10" teen, who is the son of one of players, wanted me to spend time with him in a program—what a joy and an honor!

I have driven for hours to watch Grant Willis football in Alabama. Why? I know that showing inte open doors to influence his life.

My greatest pleasure is spending time with my Teaching Lex, Ashley, Chloe and Allyson how to in my backyard is a thrill for me. Quite honestly, reason I spent money to put a glass backboard at the driveway. I even bought four basketballs—one for e

I have impacted their lives for Christ by taking th overseas, Christmas shopping in New York City, and

Recently, while Pat was out of town, I decided to do something at would make a memory. I rented a limo to take the grandchildren dinner. I called Robyn and asked her to bring Ashley and Allyson to onda's house. When the white stretch limo pulled up to the house, four grandchildren were standing on the porch. Expecting to see me celebrity, my grandchildren ran out to the car as the chauffeur ened the door—and out popped Paw-Paw!

After giving each of them a basket of toys, candy, and school plies, we headed off to Dalton, Georgia, to eat at Red Lobster. The tire evening was a blast that cost me about $400, which is why I ited for Pat to be out of town! I was glad that Robyn and Rhonda wed up at the restaurant to help me handle them, but I would not my daughters ride in the limo.

"Paw-Paw, you're cool!" Lex exclaimed at the end of the evening. ssion accomplished!

For years I coached college basketball. I enjoyed the relationships h my players so I continue to coach and develop winners. My greatest or in life is to know that I have influenced and made an impact on e young life. Making a difference in another life gives me a sense of ning and purpose. Because of all the influences and contributions ple made in my life, I feel compelled to give myself to others. This is passion.

Coaches must connect with their players. Without good munication, the team will be confused about its mission. Whenever ach develops his game plan, selling the strategy to each member he team involves competence, confidence, and connecting. True ection depends on trust and results in the bonding of hearts and ds. Such a connection cements a relationship and makes a distinctive defining difference in the quest to influence and impact others.

194

Unless we learn to establish good relationships and connect with others, we will never effectively contribute to their success.

• • • •

West Virginia is an interesting state. Soon after I started SCORE International, friends in West Virginia threw a party for me at the home of Olen and Fran Doddridge. Composed mostly of members of Antioch Baptist Church, these friends gave me a computer, which at the time was a huge, expensive gift. Through the untiring, enthusiastic leadership of Dennis Mills, those West Virginia people became the source of continuous giving that helped launch the worldwide ministry of SCORE International.

Fifteen years later, an Italian hotel owner in the Dominican Republic offered to sell me his hotel. At first, I was stunned by the idea—since I had no money. SCORE International had no assets, and the thought of buying a hotel in a foreign country seemed like a joke.

Looking at the financial sheets of our ministry, I discovered we were paying a huge amount of money to keep our teams in hotels. I began to understand that the money could be used to make payments on our own hotel.

I began to pray, and God demonstrated His glory to me. Guy Willis, a lawyer in Alabama, gave a significant gift toward the project. Another lawyer in Alabama heard from Guy about our plan and donated a title deed to his house, which he had placed on the market to sell. Another friend, Wally Pittman, sent a significant gift. Finally, Jeff Hoops, from West Virginia, gave us a new house which appraised at $278,000.

God used these three men to generate over $300,000, which was the foundation for ownership of the hotel.

Today, in the Dominican Republic, SCORE International owns a hotel, land, a dental/medical clinic, two tour buses, a van, and three cars. With these assets, we are able to host groups from the USA and use this base to train students in missions.

Guy, Wally, and Jeff have continued their generosity to our ministry. All of them are very unique people, who have become my good friends.

I met Guy at Heritage Baptist Church in Alabama. One night after church, he invited me to go to a restaurant for coffee and dessert. He was wearing a white T-shirt and jeans. I thought he was a truck driver or mechanic. When I was told by his pastor, Roger Parks, that he was a lawyer, I was shocked.

Guy, wife Debby, son Grant, and daughter Bethany have become close friends. In 2004, Pat and I took our granddaughter Ashley, along with the Willis family, to New York City during Christmas week. Ashley and Bethany spent time (and our money) at the American Girl near our hotel, off Madison Avenue. I love to be with Grant, who is a great athlete.

Wally is another great guy. We are both very competitive. He became very successful by founding a newspaper, featuring ads for buying and selling. We met at his church in Virginia. When Wally discovered I was a golfer, he asked me to play. Playing with Wally, Paul (his son), and music evangelist Mark Chaney, I found out how competitive Wally really was. Paul was only 14 at the time. He was just learning to play, and Wally was very impatient with him. Wally is a perfectionist who wants everything to go just right. When Paul struggled, Wally pushed him hard. Riding in my cart, I told Paul not to worry but to enjoy the game.

Paul became my friend! We always played as partners against Wally and whomever. I sought to give Paul confidence and encouraged him to concentrate on getting better. He did just that! Paul became a very good golfer, and we became best of friends throughout his teenage years. Later, Paul married Kelly, a beautiful girl, whom he met at Liberty University. I was the minister for their wedding ceremony.

Betty and Wally Pittman have given a lot of resources to our ministry. Pat and I treasure their friendship. I often think they fell in love with us because we fell in love with their son.

Jeff and Trish Hoops met me at Bible Baptist Church in West Virginia. Jeff, a coal mining executive, was intrigued by my sports ministry. He signed up to go on a missions trip with me to Russia. With his last name and love of sports, Jeff became a natural for the basketball delegation to share the Gospel.

I still remember taking a great USA team with three NBA first-round draft picks. We played in front of thousands of Russians each night. Jeff and others gave enough money for us to take fifty-thousand Bibles to distribute at the games.

When I go to West Virginia, I stay with either the Hoops or the Doddridges. While staying at Jeff and Trish's house on one visit, I encountered a dilemma. When I got ready to go to a country church in the West Virginia mountains, I discovered that the Hoops could not go; however, they said I could drive one of their cars. Looking in the garage, I saw a white Hummer and a new red Corvette. What a decision! I told Jeff that I could not drive a Hummer or Corvette to a country church, since it would kill my love offering. Instead, I chose the S-10 farm pickup truck.

These three families became the most generous people supporting our ministry, but the love and friendship of such wonderful friends in West Virginia have become the real backbone of our work. I have my own room when I visit the Doddridges. Dennis Mills has been God's man to connect me to so many donors. He has worked hard to make my name known to churches in those hills. Fred Bias, another West Virginian, has raised tens of thousands of dollars for our orphanage in the Dominican Republic. We would have never bought a new bus if Olen Doddridge had not complained so much about the old, yellow, school bus that broke down each time he rode on it.

I cherish all the Rook games with Tennis and Kathy Adkins. Kathy's cookies contributed to my clogged arteries. So many West Virginians have helped me—people such as C. J. Nicely, Pastor Bill Davis, Merle Jefferson, Jack Midkiff, and Jerry Hatfield.

Steve and Marty Johnson are two more West Virginians who have been my friends. They are brothers and partners in the food–store business. Steve and Faith have a love for missions. God used them to get me interested in Jamaican projects. Marty and Frances are very involved in our medical ministry in the Dominican Republic. Both families have participated in numerous missions trips and have given generously to the ministry. Steve and Marty are board members of SCORE International.

Relationships are vital to me. I am a people person. I want to make an impact upon others. My desire is to make a spiritual difference in the people around me.

Years ago, God called me into the ministry. I had little to offer—no assets or resources. However, God brought hundreds of people into my life. From California to Florida, God has given me friends. Relationships are pivotal to a man's success—People really matter. People who share your values, your lifestyle, and your desire to serve God contribute greatly to your success.

No player ever won a team championship without the support and contribution of teammates. A championship is won by the collective contributions of every member of the team. To be successful, the MVP or CEO must recognize and appreciate the impact of others.

CHAPTER 20

TOP TEN MINISTRY MOMENTS

Recalling my greatest moments of ministry proves challenging. More difficult, however, is evaluating those moments in the light of eternity. I will only be able to enumerate what was meaningful to me. For instance, speaking at THE WILDS, a youth camp in North Carolina, would never rank in my top ten list. However, Chip DeArmon trusted Christ at that meeting and later became senior pastor of a large church in Florida. I spoke at a Christian school in Atlanta which no longer exists. But in that chapel, Bruce Kehlenhofer received Christ. He later became missions pastor at a megachurch in Jacksonville, Florida.

I will list ten of my most memorable moments in ministry. However, some day in Heaven, I hope to meet a lot of people who may argue these points, since I never saw the impact on this side of eternity. Anyway, here is the list.

1. **Preaching in Russia**. I would have to say that preaching in Russia in 1992 after the fall of Communism ranks at the top. I preached to thousands of people who had not heard a clear public presentation of the Gospel in their lifetime. It was thrilling to see people follow me every day and ask for a copy of the Bible.

2. **Communicating the Gospel to millions in Mexico on television**. In Mexico, one cannot buy time on television to preach the Gospel; however, from Pachuca, the Mexicans televised our basketball game to Mexico City. Since we had signed agreements that allowed us to preach at the halftime of the game, we were able to share about Jesus to millions of people watching the televised game.

3. **Speaking at a Tennessee Temple graduation**. Few people ever have the opportunity to preach at their college alma mater. Tennessee Temple College will always be special to me. There, I received my college education, a Master's Degree from seminary, and served on the faculty. I met my wife, Pat, at the college. I will always cherish the honor to speak at a Tennessee Temple graduation. I only spoke for 13 minutes. I remember telling the students that I never remembered any speaker or his topic at any of my graduations. I knew they were not there to hear me. They would not remember me or anything I said. Well, I was wrong. I still have people come to me and tell me that they remember me speaking at their graduation. What they remember is that "I only spoke 13 minutes." At that graduation, the college gave me an honorary doctorate degree.

4. **Preaching in Dominican Republic when Rhonda got saved**. I have preached scores of times in the Dominican, but one night is the most memorable. I recall that the lights went out in the building as I began my sermon. Preaching in the dark in a foreign country can be intimidating. During the invitation, someone touched me—

my youngest daughter, Rhonda! She was weeping as she threw her arms around my neck. In the Dominican darkness, the light of the Gospel had reached the heart of my little girl. This was a very special moment.

5. **Watching 696 teenagers respond to my message at the United Center in Chicago**. After an NBA game between Dallas and Chicago, I preached to several thousand teenagers invited to the arena by hundreds of churches. The event sponsored by Word of Life is called Superbowl. God anointed the message that night. Throngs of teens responded to receive Christ. The leaders of the event later gave the results, 696 teens saved. Wow! On that evening, the Lord Jesus Christ was truly exalted as the "FAMOUS ONE, " not Michael Jordan.

6. **Preaching at the Woodland Park Baptist Church Missions Conference**. I have been honored to preach at many missions conferences. Some of the largest and greatest churches in America have invited me as their Keynote speaker. However, none will compare with the conference at my home church in 2005. I had been scheduled to speak a year in advance. No one knew that I would have heart bypass surgery and a blood clot in the leg just a few weeks before this scheduled conference. Pastor John Meador gave me an opportunity to opt out of this engagement. After all, it meant that I would preach three times on one Sunday. I knew that two of our most famous members might be present. Author and internationally known speaker, Kay Arthur, is a member of WPBC, along with Dr. Spiros Zodhiates, a famous Greek scholar. Both intimidated me. I was physically weak, but I knew I wanted to speak. I had a message to give. I was just being obedient to God; besides, I understood it would be the right thing to do as well as

therapeutic for me. God empowered me and energized me that day to share my new heart with God's people. I will always treasure that moment!

7. **Preaching under the anointing at Calvary Baptist Church**. During my tenure at Calvary Baptist Church in Chattanooga, Pastor Kelton Williams asked me to preach a message. God gave me a sermon on Job entitled, "When the Dust Settles!" I have preached thousands of sermons. I do not recall a time in my ministry when the anointing of God's Spirit was on my preaching as it was on this occasion. It was a message of encouragement. Job had suffered so much adversity, but "when the dust settled," he proclaimed his determination to walk with God. It was the right message at the right time for the right people. God walked into the service that night! The anointing was so real that I could not give the sermon a proper ending. I simply walked off the platform as the people stood, shouting, clapping, crying, and praising God. We had clearly been in the presence of Jehovah that day. I have prayed many times for a duplication of that moment, but those times are rare and will always be special reminders—that it is not the speaker but the Sovereign One who authors those moments.

8. **Missions Conference in Argentina at Word of Life Bible Institute**. Jerry Walls and I traveled to Argentina to speak at the Annual Missions conference at Word of Life. More than five-hundred Hispanic students were in attendance, along with approximately fifty bi-lingual students from the USA. God spoke to hearts, and over two-hundred students responded to the call of God by walking forward to commit their lives to be career missionaries. I remember praying with a young lady from Gainesville, Georgia. Allison McGill was afraid to go home and tell her parents about her

decisions. Her parents were physicians and planned for Allison to follow them in the field of medicine. God not only sent Allison, but her parents were so moved by her decision that they went on a short term missions trip. During that trip, the Lord spoke to them. They returned to Gainesville, sold their practice, divested, and committed to do missions work. Today, Allison is married and serving overseas. Her parents are missionaries in Bolivia.

9. **Citywide crusade in my hometown**. Preaching in your home area is always tough. I was invited by the ministerial association of Blacksburg to preach in their Annual Citywide crusade. God saved my parents at this crusade in 1962 and challenged me to dedicate my life to Him. In the late 1990s, I was invited back to preach that crusade in my hometown. Wayne Brown, a classmate who is a pastor, led the singing and I preached. We had a great time! Many people came to listen to these homegrown preachers. Some of the audience intimidated me a little. Some of my high school teammates, a couple of girlfriends, and a few friends who knew some real "stuff" about me were present. I was determined to meet all of them at the altar!

10. **Speaking at the Inauguration of Joe Jordan**. When I was in college, I remember spending time with my teammate, Joe Jordan. Joe and I had similar home situations as teenagers. One night on our way to a game, Joe and I spent time discussing our future. Both of us determined to make our life and ministry count for God. Years later, Joe was named Executive Director of Word of Life International. At his inauguration, I was invited as one of several speakers. I remember sitting next to Dr. Charles Ryrie, the renowned theologian. Other great men sat on the platform. This experience humbled me, but I cherished this holy moment of laying hands on a teammate, as he

began his leadership of one of the world's greatest youth ministries. I was so proud of Joe.

There have been many great victories in my life. I can never adequately describe the thrill of winning a national championship. Being a champion in sports is the ultimate dream of every athlete. However, the great moments of ministry will be cause to rejoice throughout eternity, while the temporal trophies gather dust in the attics.

The vision that God cast in my heart to become a winner in life will always be clear. Chasing that vision has been the passion and purpose of my life. These ministry moments are simply laps in that winning race.

A FAITHFUL FINISH

CHAPTER 21

IMPACTING FRIENDSHIPS

I have always been a "people person." I just love people. I have always viewed my work as a people ministry. Every CEO, administrator, politician, pastor, or coach needs good people skills. Strong leadership is a key to success since "everything rises or falls on leadership". Understanding and caring for people makes a difference.

While coaching, I recruited a great group of players. People such as Allen Carden, Paul Pridemore, Tommy McMasters, Anthony Eubanks, Mark Trammell, Benny Polk, David Montgomery, Archie Barnes, Kevin Hicks, Jeff Smith, J.R. Lucas, and so many more were a delight for me to be around. These guys had character and spiritual direction in their lives. The class that I inherited from Bruce Foster was a solid group. Players such as Jerry Adams, Mitch Steiner, Dan Smith, Victor Hazard, Jim Shoemate, Jim Hubbard, Paul Zahn, and Tony Phelps were good students, excellent players, and campus leaders. These players made our student body proud, and students enjoyed being around them.

I loved working with Randy Smith. He became a special person in my life and career. Randy asked me to help him televise college basketball games as a color commentator. Randy and I were so different! Randy was a Methodist and a diehard Democrat. When we met, he would drink an occasional glass of wine and even cuss a little, but we became close friends. I saw God work in his life. We talked about the Bible and prayed together. Randy even invited me to speak in his Methodist church in Whitwell, Tennessee. He and his wife, Sheila, were devoted to their children and had a strong marriage. Randy and I became close friends, even though we argued heatedly about Bill Clinton and the rest of his Democratic politicians.

Randy taught me the ropes of television. We enjoyed doing more than 120 games together. I took Randy and a television camera man to Argentina to do a documentary on our sports evangelism ministry. They came to Buenos Aires a couple of days after my arrival. As a matter of fact, when they flew into the country, I forgot to meet them at the airport. I was caught up in an intense tennis match with my good friend, Joe Jordan, at Word of Life. Randy and David Moore, the camera men, sat at Ezeiza Airport for 4 hours until I remembered their schedule. They had no Argentine money, no food, and no understanding of the Spanish language. The fact that David is Afro-American and no black people live in Argentina only added to the drama. He attracted a lot of stares and gawking from the Argentine people at the airport.
It is amazing that we are still close friends today. God used Randy Smith to impact my life in incredible ways.

Sam Woolwine was another person who contributed heavily to my success as a coach. Sam was a sports writer at the local newspaper. He later became the sports editor. Almost every week during our basketball season, Sam printed numerous articles about our team. The articles were large and the pictures were often in color. Sam was assigned to cover Tennessee Temple University. He even went on a three-game road trip with us to California. With articles and pictures of me in the newspaper and television coverage from Randy Smith, I received a lot of recognition in the city of Chattanooga.

Sam and I enjoyed more than a professional relationship. We have always been close friends. We have cried together, laughed together, and prayed together. I tried to stay close to Sam when he went through an emotional divorce. I counseled him on many occasions, concerning his children. I even officiated the wedding of his oldest daughter.

As a coach, I will always recognize the contributions of Sam Woolwine to my professional success. Publicity is so important when you seek to build a championship program. Good publicity is also an immense positive factor in recruiting. However, my friendship with Sam supersedes the professional relationship we had.

Not only did Sam and I have a good relationship, but I also cemented a relationship with his boss, Roy Exum, grandson of the newspaper publisher. Although Roy can be loud, hyper, and intimidating, we hit it off in a big way. When Roy had some misunderstanding with Murray Arnold, head coach of the University of Tennessee at Chattanooga, guess who became the beneficiary? The state university NCAA Division I team coverage was buried on the fourth page of the sports section, while Tennessee Temple received front-page headlines with color pictures. Roy and I were friends, and I always stayed on his good side and learned to "play ball" with him.

Another writer later assigned to cover us was Ron Bush. Ron was also a friend. I spoke in his church and officiated at his wedding.

Sam, Roy, and Ron were professionals whom I knew could provide print publicity to present my program to the metropolitan Chattanooga population of over three-hundred-thousand people. However, I cherished their personal friendships more than any publicity.

Friends contribute to one's success! No one ever got to the top without surrounding himself with impacting relationships.

One of the greatest lessons that I have learned in life is that a man's success or failure is determined by the friends he chooses. People are vital to success. Relationships, partnerships, and friendships assist men in their quest for success. Being surrounded by key people, good people, and successful people helps a driven person to accomplish his goals in life. One should have high standards for the people who come into his life.

Hillary Clinton once talked about how "it takes a village" to impact a person. While I am not a fan of Mrs. Clinton, she was right. Every successful person needs an entire village of people surrounding him in order to establish goals, climb ladders, and achieve success!

• • • •

Jerry Walls, Gordon Godfrey, and Doug Ripley have been part of "my village." These pastors have been a source of constant encouragement to me and my family. They have always been there to meet my needs. I have leaned on them for words of wisdom and advice. I speak to them every week. These are trustworthy friends who are loyal to me and my family.

Jerry and Willie Pace were my favorite students when I taught at Tennessee Temple University. I taught a class called "Coaching Basketball." Most of my players were in the class. Jerry and Willie took a lot of physical education classes, and they signed up to take this class. Both were great athletes in Montgomery, Alabama. I took a real liking to these guys. Every day, they went to the Happy Corner to buy me a cup of coffee. Naturally, both got A's in my class!

Today, Jerry and Willie are successful pastors of great churches. I have preached many times for both of them. We have traveled overseas on missions trips together. I know Jerry and Willie love me, support me, and pray for me. Every servant of God needs to find a shoulder to cry upon, an ear to listen, and a heart to help. I will never forget when I had open heart surgery—Jerry was right there with my family.

Gordon is a man short in stature but is a giant in spiritual leadership. This man is gifted in church growth, leadership skills, administration, and finances. Many times I have called Gordon in a time of great need. Every time, God has used Gordon to connect me to resources that have enabled me to continue the work. I have spoken in his church many times. The fact that his people have expressed great affection for me is a reflection of his loyalty to me.

Doug is another super friend and great advisor. Doug has held me accountable in the area of ministry. He will not allow me to drift. Of all the pastors I know, he has the greatest heart for missions. We have walked through tough valleys together. When I am down, I know I can always count on Doug. He has always lifted me up.

These men are true friends. I have needed them and they have demonstrated how true friends can meet needs. Job had a lot of trials and trouble. His friends judged him, condemned him, and discouraged him. I am glad Jerry, Gordon, and Doug are the complete opposite of the friends that Job had.

Finally, I cannot fail to mention my hero. Every man needs a hero that he can model. Charles Barkley was completely, absolutely wrong to express that he is no role model. He is! He is a role model because of the talent God gave him and because of the generation that placed him on a pedestal. Unfortunately, Charles Barkley is a BAD role model.

I have had great role models in my life. Dr. Lee Roberson tops my list.

Dr. Roberson is the greatest man of God I ever knew. He is the epitome of integrity. Dr. Roberson showed me a life of consistency, courage, and conviction. He NEVER strayed from his commitment. He always wore a dark, double-breasted suit. He never went to a mall. He was never late! He demonstrated great leadership. He was never distracted from his mission in life. Though his topical preaching style was simplistic, Dr. Lee Roberson was a powerful voice in the fundamentalist movement.

People contribute to the success or failure of a life and ministry. In my quest for success, I am grateful to every person who came into my life. People have enriched my life, energized me, and edified me in spiritual things. As a result, I have drawn strength to attempt great things for God.

CHAPTER 22

BIBLICAL PERSPECTIVE OF SUCCESS

I value winning because I know what it is like to be a loser. Above every accomplishment I have achieved in life, my greatest area of success has been my family. As I observe many failures in family, I am most thankful to have a family that honors God. My wife, Pat, shared my vision from our first date. She has been my greatest inspiration and the most committed Christian I know. She is the reason for my success.

Our daughters, Robyn and Rhonda, have been a huge blessing in our home. They never did anything to embarrass us. They lived consistent Christian lives. Though they were totally different, they shared common goals. Raised in a preacher's home, both girls embraced our values and honored me with their commitment to a Christian lifestyle. They were good and Godly!

Both daughters married good men. Greg serves as a deacon in our church. Tim works in the ministry of SCORE International. They are godly husbands and great fathers. Our daughters birthed two children each. Robyn and Greg have Ashley and Allyson. Rhonda and Tim have Lex (my only grandson) and Chloe. Ashley is the oldest, and she is a great student and loves the things of God. The other three grandchildren are young and are interested in church, Awana, and learning more about God and His Word. I love my grandchildren. They have brought to my life blessing, joy, and love.

Basketball, preaching, television, and SCORE International have been huge areas of dedication in my life. However, I am the proudest of the victories and success that God has given Pat and me in raising, mentoring, and sharing a family.

Any success in any area of my life must be attributed to the grace and goodness of God. God's hand on my life has guided me to be a champion. He has directed my path. I cannot explain my life any other way. Doing God's will has transformed an average, small-town boy, with no advantages, to realizing success, based on eternal values.

Glory to God!

• • • •

Success is biblically defined by Joshua 1: 8. Finances, fame, friends, and family do not equal success. Sometimes, success comes in spite of all! Being inducted into four halls-of-fame does not define success. God's fervor in our lives defines success. God's fervor sees us through the dark house of desertion by those close to us, the depression that follows our short-comings, and the discouragement when we encounter setbacks. Success is not without losing, falling, or tears. It is all about the passion to sail on, pursuing the light of another day to honor our Lord and enjoy Him forever.

My greatest image of success is seen in the lives of three Old Testament men—Joseph, Joshua, and Nehemiah. They were all <u>real</u> men and <u>real</u> leaders.

With these men I see three common traits—integrity, vision, and leadership. They are the very foundation to success.

<u>Integrity</u>

Real winners are men of integrity. Joseph was a man of integrity. In Genesis 39:2, the Bible states that "the Lord was with Joseph, and he was a <u>prosperous</u> man,!" The fact that "the Lord was with him" was obvious to all around him. Because of his integrity, the Bible states that "the blessing of the Lord was on all that he had in his house, and in the field" (Genesis 39:5).

Joseph demonstrated his integrity by refusing the tempting sexual advances of Potiphar's wife. This seduction was real, and the enticement was strong. Because of his moral and spiritual integrity and the passion to "do what was right," Joseph maintained his integrity.

Doing the right thing is always the bedrock of one's integrity. In our culture, people abuse and offend others for personal advancement. We see this in business when a person leaves a company to start another competing company down the road, appealing to the same customers. In the professional world, legal agreements have to be designed with a "no compete clause."

Coaches who lack integrity pursue players who have committed to other colleges, even though they have not signed. Athletic directors who lack integrity pursue successful coaches under contract at competing schools, without seeking permission from the college with which they signed contracts. These things show a lack of integrity.

Sadly, some pastors and missionaries do the same. They may take disgruntled believers from a church and organize that group in a church just a few miles down the highway. Sometimes believers in Christian work act like the pagans in the business world. Those who do such things lack integrity. While they may appear to be successful, the work will not stand that is built on such a foundation.

When I left Bethel Baptist Church, I determined to do it the right way. That's why I told the paper that if they ran the article before I spoke to the church, I would not resign. That was the right thing to do for the wonderful people at Bethel Baptist. Years later, I served as interim pastor at Calvary Baptist Church in Chattanooga. Many pressured me to be a candidate for the pastorate. The church had an average of 550 people in church and over $2 million in the bank. As long as I stayed there, no one would get the 75 percent vote to become the new pastor. I knew that I could get that vote, but we would lose fifty to one-hundred people. What should I do? It was tempting! I knew I could survive a power struggle, because I had a lot of support behind me. However, that would NOT BE THE RIGHT THING for me or the church. I was hired to be "interim" pastor after serving 10 years as the assistant pastor. With an understanding of my role, I would have been wrong to aspire for the position. Therefore, I did the right thing! I resigned and left the church. Several months later, the church called Steve Roberson, a former player and a friend. The church grew and our ministry at SCORE flourished.

Selfish agendas will never attract the favor of God. God honors those who honor Him with integrity. God always prospers those who determine to do the right things.

God was "with Joseph." This was obvious to everyone, even to those who despised him, abandoned him, lied about him, and tried to destroy him. Yet, Joseph extended grace to his brothers, forgave them, and nourished them (Genesis 50:21). What they meant for evil, God turned into good, because God <u>always</u> honors men of integrity.

Dr. Bob Jones Sr. always said, "Do right even if the stars fall!" We must reject the temptation to advance ourselves, achieve our agenda, and aspire to build our kingdom at the expense of others. Joseph reached out to those who offended him for 17 years. Can you imagine having your own relatives seeking to bury you and your ministry? This happened to Joseph, yet he kept reaching out, encouraging them, and kindly caring for their needs—What integrity! No wonder God favored him. He will always advance and prosper men of integrity. Do right!

Vision

Joshua was a man of vision. He was sent with a team of spies to scout out the land. The team came back with facts. Ten members of the team formed a majority to report that the land was fortified and had giants living there. In Numbers 13 and 14, these facts are recorded. However, only two men faced the facts with faith. Joshua and Caleb stood tall against the majority report to declare that the land flowed with milk and honey.

In Numbers 14:9, Joshua declared, "The Lord is with us, do not fear them (the enemy)." Basically, Joshua was saying, "We can do it!" Joshua was a man of vision. His focus was on the opportunity and not the opposition. By faith, Joshua saw the victory.

The team was dead wrong! The majority may rule, but it is not always right. Boards are good for sharing views, gleaning wisdom, and holding leaders accountable, but God always raises a leader for others to follow. Every team needs a point man for leadership. A team is not a democracy. Joshua had a vision from God, took responsibility, made bold decisions, and made himself accountable to others.

Without vision, one wallows in the mire of mediocrity. Great Biblical leaders were men of faith and vision. Wise enough to listen to others, bold enough to make decisions, and willing enough to be accountable to others, men of vision became men of action. As they cast their vision on others, visionaries connect with winners who desire to make a difference in the Kingdom.

Leadership

Every successful coach, player, businessman, and pastor must be a strong leader to achieve great accomplishments. A coach must be a strong leader for his team. He cannot rely on the team for vision. A businessman must make strong decisions to build a company that thrives. Likewise, a pastor must have the courage to lead the ministry he wants to accomplish.

In the Bible, Nehemiah was a true leader with strong convictions. After viewing the ruins of the walls at Jerusalem, he sat down and wept. However, he did not remain there long. After communion with God, Nehemiah took his plan to the king. The conviction was simple: Nehemiah had a passion to rebuild the walls of Jerusalem so that God's people would no longer be a reproach.

The king granted his wish because he saw the good hand of God upon Nehemiah (Nehemiah 2:8). After seeing the ruins again, Nehemiah summoned a team and began to lead them. His leadership was so strong that they exclaimed, "Let us arise and build" (2:18).

There are several principles found in the first two chapters of Nehemiah.

Principle # One: God executes His plan through a man—not a committee, a board, or a team.

Principle # Two: God confirms His plan to others.

Principle # Three: Man must pass the plan to other potential leaders.

Principle # Four: Conviction will always be followed by opposition.

In the case of Nehemiah, opposition came from Sanballat and Tobiah.

One should note that when God begins to execute His plan, voices of the enemy begin to resonate. No sooner had Nehemiah shared his conviction with his friends in Nehemiah 2:18 that the voices of the enemy echoed with scorn. Those voices became more intense as the plan began to evolve into organized action. Basically, Nehemiah heard three voices.

First of all, there was the voice of <u>intimidation</u>. In Nehemiah 4:1, the enemy was mad and began to mock the Jews when they saw the work begin. Their anger and mockery was intended to intimidate the workers. As believers anywhere begin to invade enemy territory to accomplish the vision God gives, great intimidation will arise against God's people. Athletes call it "trash-talking." The devil is a master of trash-talking the vision and ministry God gives!

Secondly, there was the voice of <u>insult</u>. In Nehemiah 4:3, the enemy scornfully stated that the wall they were building would fall if a fox climbed upon it. What a ridiculous statement! That wall was wide enough for a chariot. This statement was intended to be a humorous insult. As we venture out to realize the plan that God gives us, our enemy often whispers insults into our ears.

Thirdly, there was the voice of <u>inadequacy</u>. As the work progresses, the devil seeks to tell us that we are not capable of doing the work. His voice screams out to us that we cannot finish, we do not have the strength, and we are completely inadequate for the God's task. To be honest, THIS IS TRUE! We are weak and unable. We are also inadequate to do the work of God. In Nehemiah 4:10, Judah listened to the voice of inadequacy and said, "We are not able to do it!"

Nehemiah refused to listen to these voices, however. He knew that the voice of the enemy always follows the plan of God. He knew they could not prevail without recognizing God. Nehemiah reminded the dejected people, who were focusing on the voices of the enemy rather than the plans of God, to be fearless and faithful to the plan (Nehemiah 4:14).

"Remember the Lord!" he said.

In the New Testament, Paul said, "I can do all things through Christ who strengthens me."

Wow! What leadership! That's why every "team" needs a coach, every church needs a pastor, every nation needs a President, and every home needs a godly man. God ordained a structure of leadership—not by committee or team votes. Nehemiah was God's leader who heard the voices of the enemy, saw the discouragement of his team, but kept them focused on the plan of God.

As a player stands on the free-throw line, knowing his team is down by one point with only 2 seconds to go, he hears voices. It may be the "trash-talking" of his opponent. It could be the screams of the home crowd of his opponent, as they vocalize their insults in his ears. It could be a haunting voice, deep inside, reminding him that he missed the last two, and if he misses these, his team will lose. As the opponent calls a time out to "freeze" the shooter, coaches who are true leaders will not discuss the free throw to the shooter. They remind the team to call a time out "after we make the free throws," so the team can set the defense. Leaders remind the team, "After we make the free throws, do not foul!" We must see the victory and dispel the voices of defeat. By doing so, the shooter is released from the pressure of the moment. Nehemiah would have been a great coach, a successful businessman, and a strong pastor. He had a plan, sold it to others, faced opposition, and kept his team focused on finishing faithful. Every team must have such leadership to follow this biblical example.

True success means exerting integrity, embracing a vision, and exercising leadership. God favors men who faithfully follow His Word. As in the case of Joshua, God prospers men who honor His book. He makes their way prosperous and they "have good success" (Joshua 1:8).

CHAPTER 23

LIVING IN THE
FOURTH QUARTER

ord of Life asked me to speak at a Superbowl event in Chicago. Their evangelistic outreach would take place at an NBA arena— the United Center—following a Bulls-Mavericks game. Thousands of teens would stay after the game. Standing center-court, I would deliver the Gospel to this audience.

Speaking on the floor made famous by Michael Jordan was an honor, but God had gifted and called me to be there. So many kids use the word "awesome" to describe ordinary things. While a slam dunk by Michael Jordan may be awesome to a teenager, Jesus Christ slam dunked the whole world. Now that is awesome!

I had prepared a 15-minute message for this special event. The title was "Living in the Fourth Quarter." After all, these teens had just watched four quarters of an NBA game. That final quarter had more critical decisions, more intensity, and better overall play than the previous quarters. Everything was simply a preliminary to the grand finale.

When I announced my sermon message, a kid close to the center of the crowd cried out, "You look like you're in overtime!"

There was such a huge crowd, I never saw the kid—and it's probably a good thing. Not to be outdone, I yelled back, "Well, it beats sudden death!"

I went on to explain to the teens that there are four quarters in an NBA game. A huge clock hung over the center of the basketball court. We could watch the time ticking away. As the game got close to the end, players seemed more focused and valued the ball more. Coaches used more timeouts to communicate strategy. Decisions were magnified and seemed more crucial. Finally, a horn sounded and the game was over! No more time, no more play, no more decisions—the game was over! Someone had won and someone else had suffered an agonizing loss.

So it is with life! When a person enters the fourth quarter of life, time is precious. Opportunities suddenly diminish. Fatigue sets in. The game of life is swiftly coming to a conclusion. Winning demands good decisions. We must remember the Apostle Paul who fought a good fight, finished the course, and kept the faith.

There is only one problem!

The majority of people do not know what quarter they are living. There is no clock to tell you how much time is in the game! No one has a clue when the game of life will personally end. We don't even know what quarter we are living. One simply cannot see how much time is left. Therefore, decisions are even more crucial to success!

Speaking to those teens, I recalled my boyhood, my youth, young adulthood, and now my status as a senior citizen. God only promises a life of three-score and ten, or 70 years. Since I had lived over 55 of those promised years, I knew which quarter I was living. I drove home a simple point: No teenager in the United Center knew what quarter he or she was in.

A car wreck, cancer, shark attack, overdose, heart attack, heat exhaustion, or a drowning could mean that a 15-year-old was "in the fourth quarter" and HE NEVER KNEW IT!

I illustrated my point by giving examples of young people, children and teens, whose life had come to an unexpected end so close to its beginning. The game of life came to a swift conclusion.

My appeal was poignant. Every teen must realize that the game of life will end, and we never know when. Since we cannot watch a clock, we must live a life striving to be a winner. Making good decisions determines the winners! If the game of life prepares a soul for eternity, then accepting Jesus Christ as Savior is the greatest decision one can make. Life becomes meaningful by focusing one's life on eternal perspectives, valuing biblical precepts, and centering life on a passionate personal relationship with Christ.

That evening we saw hundreds of teens give their hearts to Christ. It was incredible—even AWESOME!

As I look over my life, I am grateful that God has allowed me to enjoy a full life. Every quarter of my life has been great. I never dreamed that a guy with my beginning, my roots, and my genetics could possibly become one of God's servants. I have always told teens that they have more advantages than I ever did to serve God. From a small town with alcoholic parents, little money, and living with grandparents on a farm, I began to see and understand the purpose that God had for my life. To be honest, I did not want to let go of my life! I had my own girlfriend, my own friends, and my own plans. God was asking me to give these things up and give it all to Him. Dying to my own plans, goals, wants, and wishes was the most difficult decision I ever made. The first quarter ended!

225

As I entered the second quarter, I met Pat. At first sight, I knew she was for me, but I had to be sure that we shared the same vision and values. Assured that we were spiritually compatible and fixed on serving Christ, we embarked on a journey that has lasted almost four decades.

The early days of marriage were a challenge. Driving an old car, living in a three-room $55-a-month apartment, and working several jobs was tough. I finished college in 1967, when Pat was just a freshman. After graduation, I began seminary, while Pat worked at the Diagnostic Center in Chattanooga. At the same time, I began my coaching career. Four years later, I graduated with a master's degree in seminary. Pat graduated from college, and our first child was born. Robyn was a bundle of joy for us.

These marked the foundational years of our lives. I eventually pastored a church in Alabama. Our second daughter, Rhonda, was born in Alabama. In just a few short years, I was a husband, a father, and a minister. The second quarter proved to be great years that molded me into the man I was to become.

Before long, it was halftime on God's playclock. I had left the Alabama church to become athletic director and head basketball coach at Tennessee Temple. Pat got her master's degree and became head of the physical education department at the university.

I enjoyed great success as a coach, but just before my turning 40, I resigned to start SCORE International. Our girls were almost teenagers when I began to travel all around the world to preach the Gospel. My little girls grew up fast, became beautiful ladies, and fell in love with two guys, who later became my sons-in-law.

Then it happened! Toward the end of the third quarter, I began to have heart problems. My first episode landed me in Memorial Hospital in Chattanooga, where Dr. Charles McDonald performed an angioplasty.

Everything went well, but it devastated me emotionally. How could this happen to me? I wasn't even 50 yet. I remembered that my dad died of a heart attack at the age of 55, and I began to wonder if I would live longer than him. Thoughts of mortality began to haunt me. I knew I was facing the fourth quarter!

Going into the fourth quarter, I became more intense in my efforts to get the Gospel to the world. Decisions had to be made about the growth of the ministry. SCORE was flourishing, but I did not want it to die when I did.

A year later, I made a trip to California. Pat and I went to Oroville to preach for Calvary Baptist Church, pastored by my good friend, Doug Taylor. After preaching five times in one day, I went back to my hotel. Late that night, I had a heart attack. I was rushed to a small-town hospital, where Dr. Glick met me in the emergency room, made decisions, and applied medicines that saved my life. Two days later, after I was stabilized, they moved me to Ensloe Hospital, a regional facility in Chico, California.

I remember meeting Dr. Swift, a cardiologist, and Dr. Rich, an anesthesiologist. I asked them if I could return home to our hospital in Chattanooga, my own doctor, and medical personnel I knew. When they gave me their prognosis and said that I may not make it back home, I consented and signed papers for the procedures. I was anxious and agitated. I wanted to go home to my family and friends. I was not a good patient! I recall when Dr. Rich came to my room and introduced himself to me, he said, "I am Dr. Rich."

I looked at him and said, "I bet you are!"

After settling me down, Dr. Swift took me to the operating room and did an angioplasty. During the procedure, the artery collapsed on the catheter, and I had another heart attack. Suddenly, as I felt like I was going to die, the artery opened and they finished the angioplasty and got the catheter out.

For five days after being released from the hospital, I lay in a hotel suite and regained some strength. I was physically and emotionally drained. I didn't have the strength to walk, but I wanted to go home!

The day we were planning to leave California to come home, Pat told me that Dr. Stephen Little had flown out to California to accompany me on the flight home. Dr. Little was a close family friend, and he wanted to be with Pat and me as we journeyed via Delta through Salt Lake City and Atlanta, before arriving in Chattanooga. Steve actually pushed me through the airports in a wheelchair.

A lot of friends were impressed that I had my own doctor fly out to California to accompany me home. I never told them Steve was a gynecologist!

When we arrived at the Chattanooga airport, I was overwhelmed by the large crowd waiting for me. Robyn and Rhonda were the first I wanted to see. Church friends, close associates, and intimate friends met me with balloons and signs. I could not hold back the tears, I felt so much love.

Yes, I got stronger! My level of intensity increased because I knew time was running out. I knew I was in the fourth quarter. I thought about it every day.

In January 2005, I finally faced open heart surgery. Because I felt so good, the news came as a shock. However, I knew this day was inevitable, considering the recurring episodes. We had held out for over 10 years, but the time had come.

I really felt good! I had no pain but a lot of questions. Why me? I actually looked forward to getting it over with. Dr. Richard Morrison was my choice to do the surgery. He was the best cardiac surgeon in Chattanooga.

The surgery went well. The next day, I was in my own private room and walking. I was in a little pain, but I was determined to obey all the orders. In four days, I went home with instructions that included walking several times a day.

Each time I got up to walk, I had extreme pain. In fact, we called the cardiac assistant twice to report the pain. Their response was that pain was part of the healing. They also recommended that I keep walking and be strong. As a former athlete, I knew how to cope with pain, and I was determined to be strong and push myself to the limit. I had seen older people than me go through this, and I was going to be tough. They told Pat not to give in to me but to make me walk.

After two weeks, I could no longer take it. I told Pat I was not going to walk. I knew Dr. Morrison was good, but he never had open-heart surgery, and he could not feel the pain I was experiencing. I refused to walk.

Pat called the doctors. They recommended coming in to check it our for our own peace of mind. After a few tests, they diagnosed a blood clot in my left leg! A blood clot! No wonder I had so much pain.
I went back into the hospital. This time, I spent eight days thinning the blood. I didn't even get out of the bed for three days. I was told that if particles of the clot broke off and went to the heart or lungs, then the game was over!!

Even though a "do not disturb" sign was placed on my door, friends still dropped in to see me. I was always grateful for friends who showed how much they cared. On the day of my surgery, I had family there to support me and dozens of people to support Pat, Robyn, and Rhonda. I received hundreds of cards and e-mails from around the world.

Kathi Freeman came to see me while I was recovering from the blood clot. Kathi and Tommy have always been special friends. Tommy is on the board of directors of SCORE International. Their children Aaron, Michael, and Danielle have been on dozens of missions trips overseas.

"Ron, you had better be careful with that blood clot," Kathi said. "My cousin had one, and when he left his hospital bed to go to the bathroom, he dropped dead."

For three days, I never went to the bathroom. I called the nurse and made them "bring the bathroom to me." I was determined to lie still in my hospital bed until the clot stabilized.

Days became weeks, weeks became months, but I got stronger. The blood clot was stabilized and the pain went away. Two weeks after I got out of the hospital, I was the keynote speaker at Woodland Park Baptist Church's missions conference. Three months after open-heart surgery, I preached at another missions conference in San Jose, Costa Rica. I was surely living in the fourth quarter, but the game wasn't over yet.

• • • •

Some people are remembered for their faults. Others are remembered by failures. Bill Buckner saw a world championship slip through his hands when a baseball went between his legs. Chris Webber lost a Final Four championship when he called a time-out, not realizing his team was out of timeouts. Barry Bonds will always be remembered for steroids and Bill Clinton for Monica.

Every person is remembered for good or bad. That is why in the last chapter of Nehemiah, three times he asks, "Oh, God, remember me." Finishing Faithful is the way to be remembered. That is the way we remember Joseph, David, and the Apostle Paul. It is the way I remember my grandmother Hardin. When spiritual values motivate our heart and mind, we can live a memorable life and do a meaningful work for God. That should be our legacy.

We are remembered by the things we value. Nehemiah valued the integrity and glory of God. He did not want the broken walls of Jerusalem to be a reproach; therefore, he led Israel in a rebuilding program. He built a legacy by doing a significant work for God which reflected his values.

Since I was a young teenager, I desired to do something for God. This desire became a driving force in my life. Spiritual battles drove the desire that defined who I really was. I would no longer allow my environment to determine my destiny. I wanted to be a WINNER!

Jesus Christ wants to make everyone a winner! He came to give us life—a winning life—because He IS the life. Life is such a precious thing, but it can be wasted. Unfortunately, many people choose to waste their lives and lose everything. Sadly, people lose their family, their health, their finances, their careers, and their will to live—usually because people choose things that destroy.

No matter what quarter of life one is in, a person must realize that life is in Christ alone. He said, "I am come that you may have life and have it more abundantly." His plan must be our passion. Only a life surrendered to Him is worth living.

Some day the final horn will sound. Time will be no more. The score will be evident for all to read. Some will win and some will lose. I choose to follow Christ and be a winner forever!

EPILOGUE

It hit me hard as I lay in the bed at Memorial Hospital in January, 2005! Recovering from open heart surgery, I decided that I had to write a book. I wanted to record my story as a legacy for my grandchildren.

I want my grandchildren to be aware of my desire to know Christ and make Him known. I want them to see how sports became a huge vehicle in my life to serve Christ. Along the journey, I have recorded a lot of stories, experiences, individuals, and divine appointments that have molded my story.

Winning has always been my goal. As an athlete, coach, minister, husband, father, friend, and servant, my objective has always been to win. I have experienced struggles, battles, defeats, hurt, and disappointments. But through all the storms, God has always brought the sunlight into my life.

This project was for my grandchildren. I am glad that you have peeked in on my life. Thanks for the time you have taken to read my story. I pray that you will see the Lord in this book. If you miss His hand in this story, you have failed to understand my story. If you see it, you will glorify our Father, Who transformed a loser into a winner.

Winning is Everything in life!